Getting Closer to Japan
Japanese Industry

Japanese Industry

William Carter

Translating Information Service Inc.

ASK Co.,Ltd.
Tokyo, Japan

Getting Closer to Japan

Japanese Industry

Copyright © 2001   by William Carter & Translating Information Service Inc.
Published in Japan by ASK Co., Ltd.
All rights reserved.

Book design by   Masami Jimbo
Illustrations by   Mari Kaneko
Editing by   Charles T. Whipple, Hiroko Kageyama, Masako Iijima,
   Mayuko Sakakibara, and Ai Ayame
Co-edited by   Translating Information Services
Supervised by   Prof. Kaoru Kobayashi (Sanno University)
DTP and printing by   SHINANO CO., LTD
ISBN 4-87217-085-7
Japanese Industry

The information included is what was available as of May 2001.
The publisher cannot be responsible for any subsequent changes in said infomation.
First edition, June 2001

Printed in Japan

Contents

Foreword

On the streets of almost any city of the world, we can find signs advertising Japanese companies and products, like Sony, Matsushita, Toyota, and Honda. And we see Japanese products in people's homes throughout the world, thanks to their good quality and reasonable prices.

When you walk along Japan's streets, you'll see people of all ages — even children — carrying cellular telephones. They are marvels of technology. And many wonder how such small, thin, and lightweight handsets could be produced.

This book gives an overview of how the Japanese industries that produce Japan's high-quality products grew from the disruption caused by WWII to be ranked as top class among the world's major industries. It will look at what drove this development and will survey conditions in various areas of the Japanese economy today.

In the 21st century, all kinds of enterprises, large and small, have begun to extend their activities across national borders. This is part of the economic globalization we hear so much about these days. Another aspect of globalization is that more and more people are coming to Japan from other parts of the world looking for jobs that fit their skills. If you are among them, this book may also give some useful information and hints about which kinds of Japanese companies might offer you the best opportunities and make the most of your skills and ideas.

Japan's economy is still in recession, more than ten years after the bursting of the economic bubble caused by the overheated economic prosperity in the late 1980s. Japan's banks are still following low-interest policies in hopes that they will stimulate individual consumption and company investments in plant & facilities. But the pace of economic recovery is still lackluster. By contrast, the U.S. economy has continued to grow ever since its recession bottomed out in the spring of 1991.

In the meantime, the whole world keeps changing. Globalization in other Asian countries, including socialist economies, has occurred rapidly. Information technology (IT) has been a motive force behind productivity and employment, and its role in overall economic growth is becoming a given.

In this global environment, Japan is striving to avoid economic crisis by trying to coordinate and improve its governmental spending and financial policies and by undertaking structural reforms in various industries, with a view to bring sustainable growth over the medium and long term. These efforts will probably bear fruit and we may expect that Japan will again, in the 21st century, be a leader in the world economy.

I would be happy if this book can further stimulate your interest in — and maybe give you some ideas for personally participating in — the various industries that support present-day Japan.

William Carter
& Translating Information Service Inc.

May 2001

Overview of Japanese Industry

Government Protection for an Industrial Superpower

The escort squadron policy

The escort squadron policy is the policy that the Japanese government adopted to help rebuild Japan's industries following WWII. Postwar Japanese industries developed and expanded under close government protection, which can be compared to the protection a convoy of ships gets from an escort squadron of cruisers and destroyers. On the other hand, the phrase escort squadron policy is sometimes used in a critical or negative sense in overseas complaints about how it might interfere with free competition.

The role of MITI

In 1954 there were over 100 Japanese manufacturers of motorcycles; today just four. This integration of the motorcycle industry came about through guidance from the Ministry of International Trade and Industry (MITI), which is now called the Ministry of Economy, Trade and Industry (METI).

One major purpose of the ministry's guidance was to make Japanese industries more competitive internationally. In part due to this guided integration as well as other government measures to protect and support exports, 80% of the global market for motorcycles now belongs to these four Japanese manufacturers, with Honda in the No. 1 spot.

In the postwar period, the government also played a leading role in building up the basic infrastructure necessary for economic recovery. Government policies dictated that the limited quantities of foreign currency and raw materials then available be concentrated in such basic industries as steel and electric power.

In 1960, the government announced its income doubling plan for the subsequent decade. As this plan materialized, Japan saw a period of especially rapid economic growth. Industrial circles made large investments in equipment and facilities, and eagerly imported technology from abroad. The steel, petrochemical, and machinery industries made giant leaps forward, and Japan's national income expanded rapidly.

Joining the advanced countries

With this rapid growth came demands, as something of a condition for joining the ranks of the world's economically advanced countries, that various trade restrictions be liberalized. Thus, the government initiated step-by-step liberalization of color TV imports in 1964, and of automobiles in 1965.

By 1972, nearly 100% of manufactured products were undergoing the first slow steps of trade liberalization. Along with this, the government continued to exercise strong leadership in efforts to restructure and integrate various industries and to help these industries' top technologies play leading roles in expanding global markets.

In the 1970s, the focus of industrial development moved from the heavy and chemical industries to knowledge-intensive industries. In leading-edge technology industries like semiconductors, new Japanese makers came abreast of, and even surpassed, established U.S. manufacturers. Almost always, such companies owed much of their success to MITI policies that supported cooperation between government and private enterprise.

This industrial development brought Japan unprecedented prosperity in the 1980s. This bullish period of Japanese economic expansion came to be known as the bubble economy. However, during this time, international trade in the form of exports grew largely as a result of protective measures — including import restrictions — aimed at nurturing domestic industries as well as policies that specifically encouraged exports. Consequently, Japan had very large trade surpluses year after year, which were met by demands from trading partners to find ways to reduce them.

Amid this criticism from abroad in the early 1990s, the economic bubble suddenly collapsed and Japan fell into a long economic slump.

Now Japan enters the 21st century with a complex economic agenda that includes plans to further eliminate excessive bureaucratic regulations and restrictions.

G o o d *to* k n o w ●

- ●ごそうせんだんほうしき［*gosō sendan hōshiki*］ ▷ escort squadron policy, convoy system
- ●しょとくばいぞうけいかく［*shotoku baizō keikaku*］ ▷ income doubling plan
- ●ちしきしゅうやくがたさんぎょう
  ［*chishiki shūyaku-gata sangyō*］ ▷ knowledge-intensive industry
- ●バブルけいざい［*baburu keizai*］ ▷ overheated/bubble economy
- ●ゆにゅうきせい［*yunyū kisei*］ ▷ import restraint/restriction
- ●ぼうえきくろじ［*bōeki kuroji*］ ▷ trade surpluses
- ●ぼうえきまさつ［*bōeki masatsu*］ ▷ trade friction

Industrial Policy and Industrial Change

Can Japanese industry shed its old skin?

From the 1990s into the opening of the 21st century, Japan went through a long tunnel of recession. Will Japan now be able to surmount the recession and find the strength to survive international competition in the new century, leaving postwar policies of industrial protection behind?

Five ways Japanese industry is changing

Since the collapse of the bubble economy, Japan's industrial structure has been changing greatly, along these trends:

(1) International specialization. Because of growing worldwide competition, many industries are moving overseas, with the obvious result that more manufactured products are being imported.

(2) Growing domestic efficiency. Fewer regulations and smaller international price differentials have given rise to growing competition, forcing domestic manufacturers to find ways to lower costs.

(3) Growing demand for services. As in other industrially advanced countries, consumer demands are shifting from "things" to "services," bringing continued growth in new service industries.

(4) Greater information content. The spread of information technology (IT: the Internet, cellular phones, TV digitalization, etc.) is changing manufacturing patterns throughout the world and Japan is no exception.

(5) Harmony with the environment — a global task. New products are being devised and manufactured with an eye to recycling and energy conservation.

A recycling society and the IT revolution

A number of government policies address these five trends. For example, in

May 2000, the Basic Law for Establishing a Recycling-based Society was passed. It brings together or replaces the separate regulations that various branches of government had made concerning waste disposal, recycling, and so on. The need to reform Japan's economic and industrial structure in environmentally friendly ways is so vital that, not surprisingly, the government is working out a number of new environment-related policies. And many are global in scope.

The government wish to promote the IT revolution as well as adjustments to the overall economy. For example, patterns of production and supply have been changed, and the role and importance of information and networking is growing.

Another important task for the government is the revision or removal of outmoded regulations and restrictions. This is being done slowly and incrementally because many manufacturers and suppliers could be doubly affected, first by recession, then by deregulation. Many of the regulations are also criticized by other countries, which would like to see a wider opening of Japanese markets.

In July 1999, the Japanese government announced its Ten-year Economic Plan, which laid out economic and societal goals to be achieved through new industrial policies by the year 2010. The plan aims for "a society of maximum freedom and minimum dissatisfaction," where individuals can freely pursue useful economic activities and protection will be given to the human rights of those who are relatively unsuccessful.

G o o d to k n o w ·

OECD economic forecast (Unit: %)

	Percentage changes from previous period			
	Adjusted total domestic demand		Adjusted GDP	
	2001	2002	2001	2002
United States	1.9	3.1	1.7	3.1
Japan	1.2	0.7	1.0	1.1
Euro area*	2.5	2.6	2.6	2.7
European Union	2.6	2.7	2.6	2.7
Total OECD	1.9	2.7	2.0	2.8

*Note: Greece entered the euro area on the 1 January 2001. In order to ensure comparability of the euro area data over time, Greece has been included in the calculation of the euro area throughout.
Source: OECD, Economic Outlook No.69, 2001

Japan's Main Industries

From textile goods to machines & automobiles

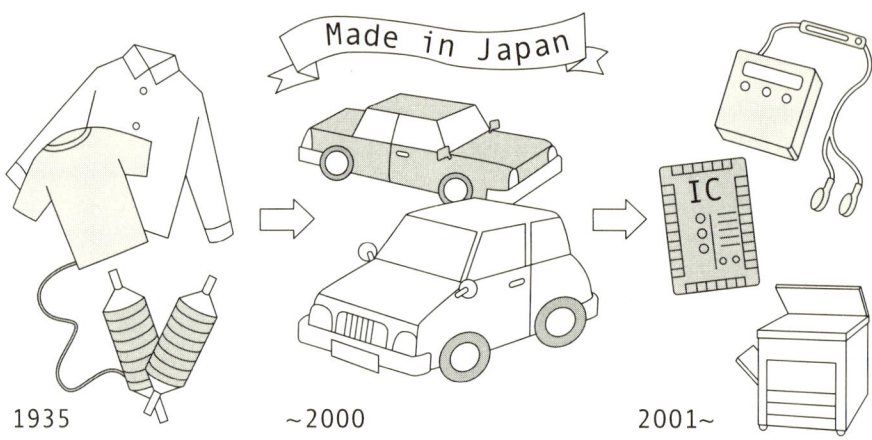

Made in Japan

1935   ~2000   2001~

In the pre-WWII years around 1935, textile products accounted for about 60% of Japan's exports. In the year 2000, textiles and textile products accounted for only 1.9% of exports while machinery was 45%, and automobiles 15%. Japan had transformed itself into a heavy-industry superpower.

The development of secondary industries

Industry is commonly divided into three sectors. Primary industries are agriculture, forestry, fisheries, and the extraction of ores, petroleum, and so forth. Secondary industries have to do with manufacturing and the processing of materials. And tertiary industries deal with services.

Since primary industries include food production, many countries see them as the most important base of their economies. In Japan, 8.1 million people were engaged in farming in 1970, but the number dropped to only about 3.2 million in 2000. During the same period, total agricultural production dropped from 4.2% to a mere 1% of the gross national product (GNP). Today much of the food Japanese people consume is imported as are grains used for animal feed.

Japan attained its important position in today's global economy because of the giant strides it made in secondary industries such as textiles, shipbuilding, steel, petrochemicals, and automobiles.

In the postwar era, the first period of rapid economic growth was from the mid-1950s to the mid-1960s, when average annual GNP growth was about 10.8%. Economic growth continued only slightly less rapidly until the first oil crisis of 1973.

Rapid changes in main industries

The world was affected by a second oil crisis in 1979. Japan depends heavily on imports of oil and other raw materials, so the crisis caused a slump among Japan's industries because of the suddenly skyrocketing prices of imported fuel and raw materials.

To overcome this problem, Japan's industry switched to fields that required sophisticated — but not necessarily energy-intensive — processing technologies. Products that used new electronic technologies were especially successful in penetrating markets throughout the world.

Although the rapid economic growth of the bubble economy ended in the early 1990s, the production of magnetic disks and integrated circuit (IC) chips remained strong, and approximately 75% of production in these categories was exported in 1998.

New growth in tertiary industries

The Ministry of Economy, Trade and Industry's white paper *Nijūisseiki no sangyō kōzō* (Industrial Structure in the 21st Century) indicates which industrial fields are expected to show the greatest growth during this century. In first place are industries related to information and communications, which are expected to grow by 100% between 2000 and 2010. Fields predicted to grow by 50% to 100% are medicine and welfare, the environment, and the movement and distribution of goods. So the Japanese economy will continue to shift away from "things" toward more and better "services."

G o o d *to* **k n o w** ··

Japan's top eight products in terms of export ratio

1	Magnetic disk equipment	76.8%		5	Color TVs	60.1%
2	IC chips	75.7%		6	Machine tools	53.8%
3	Copy machines	72.1%		7	Facsimile equipment	46.6%
4	Two-wheel vehicles	60.8%		8	Four-wheel vehicles	45.7%

Source: Ministry of Economy, Trade and Industry, An Economic White Paper 2000

Changes in Japanese Management

Japanese management in need of reform

Japanese-style management supported Japan's rapid growth and the bubble economy. It was highly praised for many years, but with the collapse of the economic bubble, increasing globalization, and the new era of heated competition, the limitations of this management system became obvious, indicating a need for reform.

Lifetime employment and the seniority system

Aiming at equaling and even surpassing Europe and the U.S., Japan's postwar managers achieved spectacular economic performance that was indeed world class in the 1980s.

Japan's distinctive management system included employment practices and relationships among companies that had characteristic features deeply rooted in Japanese culture.

Lifetime employment and the seniority system were important factors. The first virtually guaranteed employment until retirement, and the second brought almost automatic advancement in job assignments and salaries in accordance with the employee's advancing number of years with the company. Both presupposed long-term work for the same company and the building of strong inter-personal relations so that the company became a sort of family on which the employees depended for many things and toward which they maintained a high degree of loyalty.

Relationships among companies also aimed at building stable long-term relationships, most often with only a rather limited number of firms. These external relationships were similar to the interpersonal relations within a company.

This type of management brought positive results during the period of rapid economic growth, but in the later period of economic recession it became a hindrance. For example, it resulted in a lack of flexibility in responding to globalization and rapidly changing markets.

Toward a new Japanese-style management system

To create a new Japanese-style management system that can respond to the new era of great global changes involving mergers, joint-venture-based competition and technological innovations, it is no doubt necessary — as most experts now agree — to reform employment and salary systems. Thus, we see the more frequent adoption of a yearly contract system of salaries (*nempō-sei*) like those in Europe and the United States, and the more frequent employment of people who have worked for other companies.

Companies are trying to build systems where individuals can optimize their special talents and work abilities, while maintaining the successful teamwork for which the Japanese have earned a well-deserved reputation.

For Japanese companies, which have been protected in the past by a multitude of government regulations, to survive the growing global competition, they must develop the flexibility that will enable them to make decisive reforms on their own. Useful reforms might involve mergers, joint ventures, company split-ups, or other types of restructuring.

Managers must be sensitive to current consumer needs, be able to predict future needs, and be able to bring this sensitivity into play by creating practical new business activities. The new Japanese-style management systems need not copy European or American systems. If Japanese managers can build their own unique, appropriate systems, Japan will no doubt regain an effective leading position in the world economy.

G o o d *to* **k n o w** ·······························

- ●にほんがたけいえい［*nihon-gata keiei*］ ▷ Japanese-style management
- ●グローバルか［*gurōbaru-ka*］ ▷ globalization
- ●しゅうしんこよう［*shūshin koyō*］ ▷ lifetime employment
- ●ねんこうじょれつ［*nenkō joretsu*］ ▷ seniority system
- ●ていねん［*teinen*］ ▷ retirement age
- ●ねんぽうせい［*nempō-sei*］ ▷ yearly contract system of salaries
- ●がっぺい［*gappei*］ ▷ merger
- ●チームワーク［*chīmu wāku*］ ▷ teamwork
- ●じゅうなんせい［*jūnan-sei*］ ▷ flexibility

Continuing U.S.-Japan Industrial Friction

Manufacturing is still important

Over the past two or three decades, the relative importance of manufacturing in Japan's economy has declined, while that of services has increased. However, the relative weight of manufacturing is still higher in Japan than in the United States, and this gap has given rise to economic friction.

The growth
of U.S.-Japan friction

From the late 1960s into the early 1970s, the first wave of economic friction between Japan and the United States arose. During these years in Japan there was an increase in the relative weight of electrical appliances, automobiles, and other assembly-based manufacturing industries that required relatively little consumption of energy. Toyota's highly efficient "just-in-time system" of production was even adopted by U.S. factories.

In the U.S., long-predominant mass-production industries such as automobiles peaked, and there was a shift toward more technology-intensive industries. At the same time, Japanese products such as automobiles and electrical appliances flooded the American market, giving rise to imbalances in overall U.S.-Japan trade. And excellent quality and affordable prices made Japanese products very popular among Americans.

In the 1980s, U.S.-Japan trade friction became more noticeable, and some even used the term "trade war." Partly because of the appreciation of the U.S. dollar against several other major currencies, many U.S. manufacturing industries declined and there was a hollowing out of the American industrial structure. In Japan there was an even more rapid appreciation of the yen compared to other currencies, which negatively affected the international competitiveness of assembly-type industries and material-related industries. This caused a shift in Japan toward high-tech industries that produced goods with a high added value. Semiconductors played a big role and soon occupied a very important position in global markets.

In the 1990s, a hollowing out of the Japanese economy took place in the shadow, so to speak, of the bubble economy. This became more visible as the yen remained high and the recession lingered. In the United States, on the other hand, restructuring and re-engineering stopped the downward trend in the relative weight of traditionally important manufacturing industries such as steel and automobiles, helping to improve the U.S. economy. However, friction caused by the differences in the Japanese and U.S. industrial structures continued.

Sparring over Super 301

The U.S. Foreign Trade Act includes a so-called Super 301 Clause. This clause allows the American government to initiate sanctions against a trading partner judged to be damaging U.S. trade interests. In October 1994, the United States threatened to apply this clause to imports of Japanese automobiles and automotive parts. However, Japan successfully appealed the case to the World Trade Organization (WTO), arguing that the sanctions would violate WTO agreements and be contrary to the principle that governments should not interfere with markets.

Disputes caused by trade friction can now be handled more effectively through the mechanisms of the WTO than through bilateral talks alone. Except for a very few cases, such as American requests that Japan lower domestic fees for telecommunication hook-ups, the United States has refrained from taking a forceful stance in trade negotiations.

G o o d *to* k n o w ···

Japanese exports and imports in 2000, classified by region and country　　(Units: U.S.$,%)

	Exports		Imports		Balance of trade	
	Value	Ratio to SM*	Value	Ratio to SM	Value	Ratio to SM
Total	52,051,306	7.2	42,442,506	16.4	9,608,800	−20.6
U.S.A.	15,537,530	5.2	8,000,580	8.1	7,536,950	2.3
Western Europe	8,980,450	−1.5	5,752,498	5.6	3,227,952	−12.0
Australia	929,959	−1.4	1,630,380	10.3	−700,421	30.8
Latin America	2,250,399	2.4	1,196,306	5.2	1,054,093	−0.7
Asia	21,470,971	15.5	17,807,645	21.1	3,663,326	−5.7
China	3,508,833	29.2	6,286,568	23.3	−2,777,735	16.7
Asian NIES	12,244,273	12.6	5,178,351	19.6	7,065,922	7.9
Middle East	1,065,234	−1.7	5,532,530	37.6	−4,467,296	52.1
Africa	546,951	−4.9	549,992	15.4	−3,041	-
C&E Europe	283,704	18.7	658,614	19.8	−374,910	20.7
Russia	63,341	7.8	513,915	14.4	−450,574	15.4

*Note: "Ratio to SM" means "Ratio to the same month in the preceding year.
Source:"Value of Exports and Imports", April 2001 Ministry of Finance

Japanese Industry in Asia

Has Japan slipped from leadership?

With the largest concentration of industrial strength in East Asia, Japan over many years developed its trade and investment in ways that contributed greatly to what some call the miraculous growth of this region's economy. However, the Asian currency crisis that began with Thailand's baht fall of 1997 showed the limitations of the Japanese model for furthering the development of other Asian economies.

Looking to Asia for manpower

In the decades following WWII, many countries of East and Southeast Asia achieved rapid economic growth, creating what came to be known as the Asian economic miracle.

Beginning in the 1960s and 1970s in Japan, this rapid economic growth continued as a sort of chain reaction in the Asian Newly Industrializing Economies of Taiwan, South Korea, Hong Kong, and Singapore. The chain reaction then affected in China and the ASEAN (Association of Southeast Asian Nations) economies.

Japan's economic links with other Asian countries became especially important during the 1970s. At that time, Japan's domestic income levels were rising, accompanied by parallel increases in labor costs for manufacturers, and labor-intensive Japanese industries experienced a labor shortage.

Thus, many Japanese manufacturing industries, such as textiles, daily sundries, electrical and electronic parts, and the assembly of electronic devices, began investing in, and moving their manufacturing plants to other Asian countries, where wages were lower and there was a large available workforce.

Asian countries began aggressively importing foreign capital and technologies. The Newly Industrializing Economies (NIES) imported their technologies mainly from the United States and the ASEAN economies mainly from Japan. They then embarked on vigorous efforts to promote export-oriented industrialization and economic development. As the transfer of technology from Japan advanced, an Asian trade network developed and stimulated increasing trade, with Japan playing a large role.

Crisis and recovery in Asia

However, in the mid-1990s, Japan's bubble economy burst, and Japanese-style industrial organization came up against formidable barriers.

In 1997 the Asian crisis, which seemed to have been ignited by Thailand's currency difficulties, spread throughout much of the Asia Pacific Rim (less so in China). This greatly affected Japanese companies with manufacturing facilities in this region, and clearly pointed to problems that would have to be overcome in the future.

Industry in Japan and elsewhere in Pacific Asia Rim: faced a period of change. Industrial systems were reassessed and structural changes undertaken in the search for more appropriate patterns in a new era.

In 1999, it appeared that most Asian countries had overcome their crises and were poised to build a new era of Asian prosperity.

Asia's economic potential is one of the greatest in the world. The development of China with its population of well over a billion is attracting much attention, and of course Japan will continue to have a major role as a supplier of sophisticated technology that can help modernize and propel industries in China and elsewhere in Asia. Thus, Japan should give priority to reforming its own industrial structures and then work to develop new patterns for the next generation, if it intends to show more leadership in Asia.

G o o d *to* k n o w ···

GDP per capita in Japan and ASEAN countries

	US Dollars
Brunei Darussalam	14,998.00
Cambodia	2,510.00
Indonesia	1,075.00
Laos	261.00
Malaysia	3,199.00
Myanmar	3,701.23

	US Dollars
The Philippines	866.35
Singapore	21,807.24
Thailand	1,895.00
Vietnam	303.00
Japan	30,046.00

Source: International Financial Statistics of IMF, 2000

Japanese Idea Products

More than just high-tech

Japanese goods are known for high technology, high quality, and low prices. But that isn't all. There have also been some interesting and unusual idea products. Here we will discuss three such products that Japan has exported to the rest of the world.

Famikon

Sony's PlayStation, which is completely different from earlier TV game devices, became a big hit first in Japan and then around the world. The 128-bit Play-Station 2 has now appeared, with functions equivalent to those of a high-grade personal computer.

The company that originated TV games was Nintendo, with its *famirī kompyūta*, or *famikon*, which was first sold in 1983. Although it had only an 8-bit processor, it was revolutionary as a game device and soon became very popular both in Japan and overseas.

Nintendo's president, Hiroshi Yamauchi, had ordered his employees to make something that other companies couldn't

catch up with for at least a year. Because of the company's insistence on low price and high functionality, the original *famikon* kept well ahead of would-be competitors for many years.

Today, Nintendo has yielded the top position to Sony, but it is planning a comeback. Microsoft Corp. entered the game device market with XBOX, and the 21st century promises to be an era of tough competition in the TV-game field.

Instant *rāmen*

There are today many kinds of cup noodles, popular because of their good taste, low cost, and ease of preparation. The first such product was developed by the Nisshin Food Products Co. and sold to an eager public under the name of *Mahō no Rāmen* (Magic *Rāmen*). Later when domestic demand looked like it was nearing the saturation point, a man named Momofuku Ando decided to try these instant noodles overseas, hoping that even Americans and Europeans would take to using chopsticks.

The development work on the first cup noodle product was not easy. At that time, Japanese technology could not ensure a safe and problem-free product with a long shelf life, so technology was introduced from abroad. After the new product was successful in the United States, factories and markets were developed in Brazil, Europe, Hong Kong, and elsewhere.

So thanks to creative and far-seeing market strategies, cup noodles are now eaten throughout the world.

Karaoke

Today, wherever you may go, you can find people singing to the accompaniment of karaoke machines. Like TV games and instant *rāmen*, these versatile music machines were born in Japan.

In 1971, an inventor named Daisuke Inoue built the first commercial karaoke system (using 8-track audiotapes) for rental to bars and nightclubs. The response was enthusiastic, and karaoke devices were soon seen and heard in bars and clubs throughout Japan.

The technical capacities of karaoke — a coined word that means something like "virtual orchestra" — were soon upgraded and keen competition among makers brought karaoke machines with screens, moving pictures, and song-scripts by 1982, winning even greater popularity. New electronic devices enabled users to select their songs by remote control. Small, private rooms called karaoke boxes began to appear across Japan.

And the development of multimedia technology brought so-called *tsūshin karaoke* or communication karaoke, which you'll most often see today. They feature easy access, via electronic networks, to literally thousands of songs and melodies. These communication karaoke now make up more than 90% of all new karaoke devices.

G o o d *to* k n o w ·

Shipments of video-game hardware

(Unit: ¥ million)

	1997	1998	1999
PlayStation	269,000	283,166	212,484
Game Boy	142,117	107,191	73,740
Dreamcast	-	12,845	63,710
Portable-type	40,317	62,111	99,951
Others	38,900	16,983	4,740

Source: 2000 CESA Games White Paper

Japan's Pursuit of Frontier Markets

The end of 20th-century industry?

DNA

SPACE

Today Japanese industry faces the limitations of 20th-century industrial systems and is in the process of changing over to 21st-century systems. Many new industries that will be important in this new era are arising in the fields of environmental protection, information technology (IT), space technology, genetic research, and many other areas.

IT-related industries in the spotlight

Because of the Internet and the rapid development of various types of computer hardware and software, Japan's information-oriented society is quickly progressing toward a new generation. Physical distance is no longer a barrier to the movement of information between one country and another, and with the Internet, the cost and time for such movement are nearly zero.

Japan's IT-related industries are fundamental to this new world. Especially in the field of computer hardware, Japanese technology is world class.

Japan's semiconductor industry was once the largest in the world in terms of production volume. And even though that volume has declined somewhat in recent years due to competition from other East Asian countries, we now see signs of a revival. This is particularly evident in the development of semiconductors to provide added value to digitized household appliances. Experts hope that Japan will bring its traditional high technology into full play, and that the resulting new products will be affordably priced.

Environment-friendliness a priority

The world's rapid industrial development in the 20th century no doubt came at the expense of the global environment.

Japan, too, attained its rapid economic growth at the price of harm to its natural environment. However, continued economic development in the 21st century must be a sustainable coexistence between people and nature.

Recently, in Japan as in other countries, a growing number of enterprises are beginning to make environmental protection an important point in their marketing strategies. Through these so-called eco-business activities, industries are taking active roles in protecting the environment on their own initiative. It is a field in which we will surely see increasing needs in the future.

A lag in genetics-related industries

The deciphering of the human genome was nearly completed in the year 2000, thanks to worldwide cooperative efforts. As a result, there are new possibilities for curing previously incurable illnesses. Around the world, pharmaceutical and other firms have begun to develop new genetics-based products and procedures that will utilize the results of human genome research. Japan has been relatively slow to develop this field.

Staking the nation's prestige on space?

If a country has a space exploration industry, it brings together many of the most sophisticated aspects of other industries to accomplish its aims. Supposedly it increases a country's prestige if it launches satellites of its own. And some experts say that space-related markets, e.g., the development of space stations and satellites for broadcasting, communications, weather forecasting, and resources exploration and mapping, will expand greatly in the future.

Japan failed in several attempts to launch satellites with its domestically produced H-II rocket. One reason may have been repeated cuts in development funding, which seem likely to continue. Nevertheless, the government thinks Japan must launch satellites with its own rockets, for the sake of national prestige and the global reputation of Japanese industry.

G o o d *to* **k n o w** ・・・・・・・・・・・・・・・・・・・・・・・・・・・・・

- ●じょうほうかしゃかい［*jōhō-ka shakai*］　▷ information-oriented society
- ●アイティーかくめい［*aitī kakumei*］　▷ information technology revolution
- ●いでんしかんれんさんぎょう ［*idenshi kanren sangyō*］　▷ genetics-related industry
- ●こうふかかち［*kō-fuka kachi*］　▷ added value/high value added
- ●うちゅうかいはつ［*uchū kaihatsu*］　▷ space exploration

Far-out Technologies of Japan

Japan's peerless *waza*

Ferris wheel

Laptop computer

Mini-motor

Gastro-camera

With the end of the bubble economy in the early 1990s, Japan entered a period of continuing recession, and often seemed to have lost confidence. But even during this period there were clear indications that innovative technologies and good ideas about how to apply them — what some call Japanese *waza* — were alive and well.

Big things like this ...

Ferris wheels: Japan is the world's largest supplier of the Ferris wheels, named after American engineer George Ferris, who erected the first one at the 1893 World's Fair in Chicago. These huge attractions are the symbols of amusement parks and traveling carnivals everywhere. Ferris wheels have gotten bigger over the years, and in 1999 Sanoyas Hishino Meisho Corp. built Japan's largest (115 meters high) at Tokyo's Odaiba amusement park. It's a great ride, but there were also tremendous technological hurdles to be cleared, like how to stabilize the soft ground and to guarantee safety during strong winds or earthquakes.

Planetariums: About 40% of the world's planetariums, where you can enjoy close encounters with the stars and the mysterious universe, use large projectors made by Japan's Goto Optical Research Institute, which developed its first — and Japan's first — projector in 1959. For our present-day age of images, the Goto Institute is designing equipment that can project images not just of stars and space research, but also of the ocean floor, the dinosaur age, ancient human civilizations, and more.

Automated vegetable factories: If you go to a supermarket today, you can buy all kinds of vegetable any time of the year. That's possible, in part, because of the world's first automatically controlled fruit and vegetable factories, developed by Japan's Q.P. Corp. They utilize artificial light instead of the sun and sprayers to provide water and fertilizers. They can even control air flow for the optimal breeze. Factory-grown vegetables are safe and no less tasty than those grown outside.

Or little things like this ...

Laptop computers: Laptop computers — in Japanese, *nōto pasokon* (notebook-size personal computers) — are now ubiquitous, but this relatively new development began in the late 1980s. A pioneering product was the DynaBook developed by Toshiba in 1989. It was created with the same sort of idea that lay behind Sony's miniaturized Walkman audio recorder-players — to make something that could be easily carried from one place to another. Known for their high technology, Japanese *nōto pasokon* have an important place in world markets. Of particular note today are Sony's VAIO and Fujitsu's FMV-Biblo.

Cameras for stomach endoscopy: The gastrocamera, which was first developed by Olympus Optical Co., was a revolutionary tool that facilitated the diagnosis and cure of many stomach ailments without surgery. A forerunner of this technology dates back to 1950, when mirrors were attached to the end of metal probes. But the procedure proved rather dangerous. Today, miniature cameras attached to optical fibers transmit high-resolution images of the interior of the esophagus and stomach to a video screen, with virtually no risk to the patient. The same technology is being used for a variety of other applications, including archaeology and the location and rescue of buried victims of earthquakes or other such disasters.

Mini-motors: Battery-operated toys, model airplanes, and the like move with miniature motors. Many such miniature motors were first developed and brought to a high level of performance by the Mabuchi Motor Co., which today supplies over 50% of the world market for them. Originally developed as motors safe for children, similar types of mini-motors are used today to operate CD-ROM and DVD-ROM drives.

Web sites to know more about these companies

- サノヤス・ヒシノ明昌
  http://www.sanoyas.co.jp/
- 五藤光学研究所
  http://www.goto.co.jp/
- キューピー
  http://www.kewpie.co.jp/

- 東芝
  http://www.toshiba.co.jp/
- オリンパス光学工業
  http://www.olympus.co.jp/
- マブチモーター
  http://www.mabuchi-motor.co.jp/

Current Problems of Japanese Industry

Why Fewer Regulations on Japanese Industry?

Voices of criticism from the world

JAPANESE MARKET

After WWII, Japan's economy made great strides as one enterprise after another expanded sales overseas. However, there has been much criticism of Japanese barriers to imports from abroad. There are in fact various government restrictions, but in this age of global competition and changes in social structure, such over-regulation has become an unnecessary embarrassment.

Limitations of the traditional system

Japan's economy has traditionally depended on government help and guidance. And the government has traditionally intervened in private economic activities with regulations and directives.

This sort of government-industry partnership did much to assist Japan's economic growth, both before the WW II and in the half-century since the WW II ended.

However, unprecedented changes in social structure — reflecting society's continuing internationalization, the spread of information technology, and a falling birth rate — have taken place since the collapse of the bubble economy in the early 1990s. There is a new awareness that old ways of doing things are no longer appropriate, and that the old government regulations may hurt, rather than help, economic development.

With the globalization of the economy and the need to introduce more foreign capital into Japan, the Japanese government is faced with more vigorous demands to relax or remove traditional types of regulations.

Government deregulation policies

Among the issues 21st century Japan must face are environmental problems, economic globalization, the IT revolution, and a declining birth rate and a graying society.

In the years leading up to the 21st century, the government carried out three-year deregulation plans. These seem to have had a good effect in various sectors of the economy, and many voices are today calling for further deregulation to deal with remaining problems.

To cope with Japan's globalizing economy, the government must relax or remove various regulations and nurture international competitive strengths so enterprises and individuals can be more effective in world markets. The government must also make it easier for foreign enterprises to market goods and services in Japan.

To realize the IT revolution it promotes, the government must digitalize its working procedures, expand Internet and other e-commerce, and of course relax regulations on communications enterprises.

The aging of society will bring a need to liberalize regulations to promote easier access to medical information and nursing care services. Corporate pension systems must also be revised. Finally, deregulations on teacher qualifications and student recruitment may be necessary to help schools that have difficulty attracting students and to offer distinctive, individual-oriented educational experiences.

Some regulations help protect the environment

On the other hand, a certain level of regulation is needed to deal successfully with environmental problems and to protect the earth. One example is regulations on the exhaust emissions of diesel trucks in the Tokyo Metropolitan Area.

There is, however, a need to take a look at certain outmoded regulations that actually hinder the effective re-use of discarded materials and the realization of an environment-friendly, recycling-oriented society. The government today basically favors the relaxation of regulations, while recognizing the need for certain rules to protect the environment.

G o o d *to* **k n o w** ··

- ●きせいかんわ［kisei kanwa］　▷deregulation
- ●かんしどう［kan shidō］　▷government guidance
- ●えんだかさえき［endaka saeki］　▷exchange gains from the strong yen
- ●けいざいのグローバルか［keizai no gurōbaru-ka］　▷globalization of economy
- ●こくさいきょうそうりょく［kokusai kyōsō-ryoku］　▷international competitive strength
- ●じょうほうこうかい［jōhō kōkai］　▷information disclosure
- ●はいガスきせい［hai-gasu kisei］　▷emission control

How Will Japanese Firms Respond to Foreign Newcomers?

Will Japan be taken over by foreign capital?

The failed Chiyoda Mutual Life Insurance Co. was placed in the receivership of the American AIG, and the failed Kyoei Life Insurance Co. in that of Prudential — in both foreign companies. The automobile industry has seen a series of tie-ups with foreign companies, and so some Japanese are beginning to wonder if Japanese industry is becoming subordinate to foreign capital.

Foreign capital ingress

The relaxation of government restrictions has made it easier for foreign firms to set up operations in Japan, and many in the fields of information, communications, finance, insurance, and so on, have already done so.

During the bubble economy, foreign firms tended to avoid investing in Japan because of anxiety over rising land prices. This was followed by a lack of confidence in Japan's economic prospects in the immediate post-bubble period. However, after the mid-1990s, foreign capital investment rapidly increased. For example, American Family, BMS (Bristol-Myers Squibb), Compaq, GAP, Merrill Lynch, and more recently Amazon.com, decided to establish operations in Japan. Overseas capital investments in Japan rose from 369.7 billion yen in 1995 to almost 2.4 trillion yen in 1999 due mostly to a sharp increase in investments in automobiles, telecommunications, insurance, and other major sectors.

Reasons for this upswing in investment from overseas are four-fold: (1) the government's policy of relaxing restrictions is having some positive effect; (2) prices are more stable compared to the bubble period; (3) geographical distance has been overcome with the development of information and communications networks. And (4) mergers and acquisitions (M&A) involving both foreign and Japanese firms have become easier to execute.

Among the advantages foreign capital brings are new employment opportunities, the exploration of new business possibilities, and stimulation for Japanese firms to become more efficient. These are expected to be a plus for Japan's economy, and so the government is working out policies to further promote foreign capital investment.

Japanese responses

Investments in Japan by foreign companies are expected to increase and continue into the foreseeable future. This means that new competitors will appear in Japan's domestic market, and that competition will become more severe. Japanese enterprises must quickly devise countermeasures to keep abreast of this new competition.

Top priority must go to basic improvements in the internal management of Japanese companies. Employment systems will have to be reevaluated and unprofitable business lines disposed of.

Then, to compete with foreign capital, M&A opportunities must be vigorously pursued, not only to save troubled enterprises, but also for the strategic reasons of bringing in new technologies to stimulate new business growth. Many examples of this second type of M&A can already be seen in such fields as information and communications, automobiles, finance, and insurance.

Many foreign enterprises bring in management concepts that differ from those in Japan. But if skillfully applied, they may bring about some very useful managerial reforms. After all, Japan has long been good at learning from the rest of the world.

G o o d *to* k n o w ·······································

Direct investment in Japan by foreign companies, by industrial sector (Units: US$ million,%)

	FY 1998	Total for FY 1950 to 1998	
	Change from FY 1997	Value	% of total
Manufacturing industry total	12.0	27,651	45.5
Machinery	40.5	13,640	22.4
Chemicals	−48.5	8,113	13.4
Petroleum	39.4	1,344	2.2
Metals	636.4	1,587	2.6
Foods	1,013.2	828	1.4
Rubber and leather products	−75.5	597	1.0
Glass and pottery products	-	180	0.3
Textile goods	83.6	167	0.3
Others	−20.7	1,195	2.0
Non-manufacturing industry total	139.8	33,111	54.5
Trade and commerce	69.3	11,256	18.5
Services	243.5	8,800	14.5
Financing and insurance	170.9	8,596	14.1
Real estate	−17.2	2,208	3.6
Communication	393.2	584	1.0
Transportation	1,504.6	307	0.5
Construction	282.3	133	0.2
Others	22.4	1,228	2
Total	89.4	60,763	100.0

Source: Ministry of Finance / 2000 JETRO White Paper on Investments

Enterprise Restructuring

On a wave of worldwide reorganization

Today, with government deregulation in most of the world advancing, more and more mergers, acquisitions, and cooperative agreements are being made among enterprises. Of course, this wave of reorganization has come to Japan, and it seems a new company restructuring is announced nearly every day in one sector of the economy or another.

Global and Japanese restructuring

At present, worldwide communication networks and computers make it quite easy to conduct business across national borders. Thanks in part to deregulation around the world, large-scale business reorganization is taking place on a global scale, often in the form of mergers and acquisitions.

However, typical reorganizations in Japan are somewhat different from those in much of the rest of the world. The reorganization of European and American firms is done mainly as a way of putting priority investment into new activities that look toward new leaps in business profitability — in other words,

as an aggressive means to stimulate further growth. In Japan, however, what is known as restructuring — especially in response to the recession of the 1990s — has often involved mergers in which larger firms try to save failing smaller firms, typically neglecting future growth and bringing cuts in personnel.

Overcoming recession with economic development

Of course, current Japanese-style restructuring has little chance of furthering growth or increasing international competitiveness. Recently, however, some enterprises have begun to actively reorganize in growth-oriented ways.

For example, in the communications

field, the largest industry player, NTT, voluntarily began to split itself up into segments in 1999. In this way each segment could better emphasize its specialized competence, with a view to making effective advances into international markets.

To better compete with the NTT companies, the largest of the other communications companies, KDD, DDI, and IDO, merged in October 2000 to form KDDI, now the second-largest communications business in Japan. NTT, Japan Telecom, and KDDI have each formed cooperative agreements or joint ventures with large overseas communications companies, and intense competition is expected.

In the automotive industry, there have been a series of global reorganizations aimed at international joint development and the absorption of technological strengths. For example, Nissan Motor has come under the umbrella of France's Renault, while Mazda and Mitsubishi Motors are under Ford of the United States and Daimler-Chrysler, respectively.

The intensified competition for technological development among the various automotive companies and the importance they place on international development are no doubt largely in response to heightened worldwide awareness of safety and environmental issues.

Japan's financial community is now subdivided into four large groups: the Mizuho Financial Group, the Mitsubishi Tokyo Financial Group, the Mitsui-Sumitomo Group (or SMBC group), and the UFJ Group. As a sort of adjunct to this, major reorganizations in the insurance industry are also under way.

All in all, Japan's business and industry in the 21st century are seeing the birth of new organizational *keiretsu*, which are quite different from those of the 20th century.

Good *to* know ···

- ●さいへん［*saihen*］ ▷ restructuring
- ●ばいしゅう［*baishū*］ ▷ acquisition
- ●がっぺい［*gappei*］ ▷ merger
- ●ていけい［*teikei*］ ▷ cooperation/cooperative agreement
- ●けいれつ［*keiretsu*］ ▷ group of affiliated companies
- ●ぶんり［*bunri*］ ▷ split, separation
- ●じんいんせいり［*jin'in seiri*］ ▷ personnel reduction
- ●きんゆうグループ［*kin'yū gurūpu*］ ▷ financial group

How Will Japanese Industry Handle Environmental Issues?

Paying the bill for economic growth ...

During its period of rapid economic growth, Japan's economic development programs very often neglected the environment. High growth was sought with little regard for the environment of this rather small country. The price for this shortsighted approach is now having to be paid, and companies must now make investments to meet the social requirement to be more environmentally conscious.

Economic growth and environmental pollution

Starting with the Meiji Restoration of 1868, Japan embarked on a policy of intense modernization, and top priority was given to industrial development.

After the first period of economic reconstruction following WWII, Japan entered a period of rapid economic growth and a shift in emphasis from primary to secondary and tertiary industries. Development of the heavy and chemical industries replaced coal with petroleum, while energy consumption by industry and society in general rose sharply. But there was not enough awareness of the importance of protecting the natural environment.

With this rapid economic development, Japan's factories grew exponentially and their release of poisonous fumes and toxic liquid wastes into the environment caused many serious cases of air and water pollution-related maladies. One of the most serious cases was mercury pollution in Minamata Bay, Kumamoto Prefecture, which caused the debilitating

mercury poisoning called Minamata disease among local residents.

Since the 1960s, many maimed by industrial pollution took their cases to court, however, it was a long and hard way to win compensation from specific corporations for suffering caused by the pollution. The Environment Agency, which has now become the Ministry of the Environment, was created in 1971 to prevent pollution and promote the preservation of the environment.

In the 1980s, environmental issues commanded attention on a global scale. This movement pointed out how important it is for all members of the human race to become conscious of how consumption habits contribute to global warming and the destruction of the ozone layer.

In recent years, the relationship between industries and the environment has been called into further question as problems have arisen involving hormone-disrupting chemicals and other industrial wastes such as dioxins.

Toward a recycling-oriented society

As Japan advances toward becoming a recycling-oriented society, both government and private enterprise are instigating programs aimed at increasing public awareness of recycling and other ways to save energy and resources.

In 1991, a recycling law named the Law for Promotion of Effective Utilization of Resources (revised in 2000) was put into effect to oblige industrial firms to take responsibility for reducing wastes and more efficiently utilizing resources.

In April 2001, the Law for Recycling of Specified Kinds of Home Appliances — the first of its kind in the world — was put into effect. To facilitate the disposal and recycling of post-use refrigerators, TV sets, washing machines, and air conditioners, this law requires a sharing of expenses and disposal roles among consumers, local governments, retailers, manufacturers and importers.

We also see a new eco-business trend, as businesses try to use market mechanisms to help protect the environment, competing to attract customers by emphasizing the environmentally friendly characteristics of their products.

The eco-business market can be roughly divided into four categories: (1) the marketing of energy-saving materials, equipment and devices; (2) the development of products using clean energy; (3) waste-disposal services; and (4) the establishment of an environmentally friendly social infrastructure that encourages recycling and use of ecological products.

Growing numbers of enterprises are obtaining ISO 14001 certification, the international ecological manufacturing standard.

Working to resolve environmental problems is an indispensable condition for the successful restructuring of Japan's industry in the 21st century.

Good to know

- ●たいきおせん [*taiki osen*]　　▷ air pollution
- ●すいしつおだく [*suishitsu odaku*]　　▷ water pollution
- ●ちきゅうおんだんか [*chikyū ondan-ka*]　　▷ global warming
- ●かんきょうホルモン [*kankyō horumon*]　　▷ hormone disrupting chemicals
- ●じゅんかんがたしゃかい [*junkan-gata shakai*]　　▷ recycling-oriented society
- ●さんせいう [*sansei-u*]　　▷ acid rain
- ●さんぎょうはいきぶつ [*sangyō haikibutsu*]　　▷ industrial waste
- ●かんきょうにやさしい [*kankyō ni yasashii*]　　▷ environment-friendly

Prospects for Japanese Overseas Investment

Higher-quality overseas investments

To East Asia
To Southeast Asia
To U.S.A.

Most of Japan's overseas investments are in East Asia, Southeast Asia, and North America. The globalization of business stimulates overseas investments in those countries, and that competition poses certain challenges for Japan. From now on, Japanese companies must emphasize high-quality overseas investments, instead of the high-volume investments of the past, to survive and experience some degree of success.

Investing in Asia

Attracted by low-cost labor as well as by local markets, Japanese enterprises have made large investments in East and Southeast Asia, especially in China and the ASEAN countries.

Growing investments in these countries prove that Japanese enterprises have confidence in the prospects for stable economic growth in the region.

With the end of Japan's booming economy in the early part of the 1990s, the focus turned to the expanding economies in other parts of Asia. But this area of the world also soon found itself in economic crises after the devaluation of the Thai currency in 1997. The result was a sharp decline in Japanese investments there.

Among the reasons for this hesitancy to invest in Asia were (1) a lag in the relaxation of Asian governments' restrictions on foreign capital; (2) the instability of various conditions in Asian countries; and (3) the rapid growth of locally financed industry; and (4) insufficient infrastructure.

In 1999, new Japanese investments began to increase. This reflected a definite trend toward recovery in the Asian economies as well as a new pattern whereby Japanese enterprises are tending to enlarge already established subsidiaries rather than undertaking new (and often relatively small) projects.

It is only a matter of time until the technical level in countries throughout

Asia will catch up with that of Japan. This means that Japan will have to compete with its neighbors to invest in introducing new Asian-developed technology in Europe and the United States.

Expansion into Europe and America

The most frequent objectives of Japanese investments in Europe and America are to penetrate markets and to acquire new technology. The largest volume of such investments is in North America, followed by Western Europe.

Recently, increasing numbers of Japanese firms are making new investments in America and Europe. Contributing factors include relaxation of host-country government restrictions and increased competition worldwide.

In this new era of heated competition, corporate streamlining is often vital to international competitiveness. Today, an important strategy for obtaining new technologies and moving into new markets is aggressive pursuit of mergers, acquisitions, and other cooperative agreements with companies in the advanced countries of Europe and North America.

Since M&As that go beyond national borders often have immediate results, large enterprises are likely to more actively pursue such strategies in the future. For example, Japanese automotive manufacturers have begun a number of joint ventures with American and European automakers, and many similar types of joint ventures can be seen in the communications industry. Overseas expansion of this type will surely increase, particularly in manufacturing.

G o o d *to* k n o w ···

Japanese direct investment abroad, by region   (Units: U.S.$ million, %)

	FY 1998		Total for FY 1951 to FY 1998			FY 1998		Total for FY 1951 to FY 1998	
	Value	Change from FY 1997	Value	Distribution Ratio		Value	Change from FY 1997	Value	Distribution Ratio
North America	10,943	−48.8	280,806	42.7	Asia	6,528	−46.4	118,803	18.1
U.S.A	10,316	−50.3	269,713	41.0	Hong Kong	602	−13.4	17,790	2.7
Latin America	6,463	2.0	76,270	11.6	Thailand	1,371	−26.6	13,049	2.0
Cayman Islands	4,495	77.1	17,983	2.7	Singapore	636	−65.1	14,263	2.2
Panama	1,040	−7.0	25,612	3.9	Indonesia	1,076	−57.2	24,581	3.7
Brazil	466	−60.6	11,680	1.8					

Source: Ministry of Finance,2000 JETRO White Paper on Investments

Three World-Famous Businessmen

The essence of Japanese management

Panasonic

Konosuke Matsushita

Honda

Soichiro Honda

Sony

Masaru Ibuka

After WWII, Japan became a first-class industrial country largely because of the hard efforts of Japanese businesspeople and some good ideas they put into practice. Three outstanding businessmen were Konosuke Matsushita, Soichiro Honda, and Masaru Ibuka. Their personalities and concepts helped establish postwar Japanese style of management.

Konosuke Matsushita

Konosuke Matsushita (1894-1989) founded Matsushita Electric Industries in 1918 and developed it into an integrated electrical appliance maker of worldwide renown within a generation. Matsushita had several important business concepts.

First, every employee should feel the same responsibility for their work as if they were a shop or factory owner. Second, the company should be managed by the collective wisdom of many people, not dictatorially managed by one individual at the top. Third, whenever possible, information about the company's business should be made available within and without the company. Fourth, management should not be too demanding, but should have a certain flexibility. And fifth, in competing with other companies in the same field, a goal should be shared prosperity. Also, employees should be appropriately selected and given the types of work they can perform best.

He felt that profit should be thought of as a fair reward from society for the contributions to society that an enterprise makes, and that any decline in profit should be seen as an indication that more effort should be put into meeting society's needs. His motto "Peace and Happiness through Prosperity" is reflected in the PHP Research Institute that he founded.

Soichiro Honda

Soichiro Honda (1906-1991) established a small motorcycle factory in 1948, and within a generation the Honda name enjoyed worldwide fame. Through his success, Japanese motorcycles gained a reputation for unsurpassed quality. Today more than half the world's motorcycles are made by Japanese companies either in Japan or overseas.

Honda was a technical craftsman who was always young at heart. His continuing desire was to follow his hopes and dreams, and he never failed to build what he himself *wanted* to build without sacrificing quality. He emphasized creativity in the workplace and refused to subordinate his work to various government attempts to interfere with or overly regulate it. Rather like Matsushita, Honda held to the idea of making things that help people be happy, and he always kept in mind the wants and needs of his employees and customers.

Masaru Ibuka

Masaru Ibuka (1908-1997) established a small company for making electronic products in 1946. One of his partners was Akio Morita, and together they developed their small company into the Sony Corporation of global renown.

Many of Sony's products were ingeniously innovative for their time, grabbing people's minds and imaginations. Clearly, Ibuka, who was an able inventor — many say a genius — was largely responsible for Sony's success.

Ibuka's incredible sensitivity enabled him to accurately read the trends of the times, predict future needs, and develop practical technologies for imaginative products — tape recorders, transistor radios, Trinitron TVs, and miniature Walkman personal cassette player-recorders — that surprised and delighted the world.

Ibuka always concentrated on ever-more sophisticated technology and tried to maintain the high quality of Sony products. At the same time, he tried not to rush unthinkingly toward ultra-large-scale mass production, or to imitate companies that sometimes pursued profits at the expense of product quality. These important decisions helped Sony win its peerless reputation in world markets.

G o o d *to* k n o w ···

URLs for more information about Honda, Matsushita and Ibuka:

● The Story of Soichiro Honda

http://www.bspage.com/1article/peo23.html

● Matsushita: The World's Greatest Entrepreneur?

http://bus.colorado.edu/faculty/decastro/spain/matushita.html

● Masaru Ibuka

http://www.pbs.org/transistor/album1/addlbios/ibuka.html

Setting Up a Company in Japan

More and more business starts by foreigners

With economic globalization, many people from overseas are interested in setting up businesses in Japan. Now that regulations on the introduction of overseas capital have been greatly relaxed, you too might consider setting up a business in Japan.

Kabushiki-gaisha or *yūgen-gaisha*?

In legal terms, there is a difference between enterprises known as *kaisha* and undertakings known as *kojin kigyō*, or individual enterprises. Let us here talk about just the *kaisha*. In Japan, if you say "I own a *kaisha*", you are nearly sure to gain much more respect and recognition.

Although there are several types of *kaisha*, here we'll talk about *kabushiki-gaisha* (joint-stock companies) and *yūgen-gaisha* (limited-liability companies). In 1991, Japan's commercial law was revised to permit a single individual to establish a *kaisha*.

In Japan, a *kabushiki-gaisha* requires paid-in capital of at least 10 million yen.

Stocks distributed to stockholders must initially be worth at least 50 thousand yen per stock unit.

The greatest advantage of a *kabushiki-gaisha* is its potential for future development. Even starting out with a small company, it could be a large enterprise in the future if many stockholders are brought together for that purpose.

A *yūgen-gaisha* requires paid-in capital of at least 3 million yen, and less than 50 employees. Still, the *yūgen-gaisha* is well-suited for a small-scale enterprise. There can be strong relationships of personal trust among the relatively small number of employees, and the company's or the employees' unique character and individuality is more easily respected and maintained. There are also fewer legal restrictions than with *kabushiki-gaisha*.

What procedures are necessary?

For a new *kabushiki-gaisha*, you must first decide on one or more *hokkinin* (originators). For a new *yūgen-gaisha*, there is no need to designate *hokkinin*. The more general term *shain* (company member) is sufficient.

For *kabushiki-gaisha*, the *hokkinin* put together articles of incorporation known as *teikan*. These must include a statement of purpose, name of the firm, number of stocks anticipated, price per stock, number of stocks issued at the time of the company's establishment, address of company headquarters, types of advertising, and the names and addresses of each *hokkinin*. All *hokkinin* must indicate their agreement to each of these items.

The company name (*shōgō*) is basically unrestricted except that it cannot be the same as a company name already registered in the same city, town, or village.

After deciding on the nature and activities of the business, obtain the appropriate registration forms and fill out the requested information, including the name of the bank that will handle the company accounts. The procedures are finished as soon as the required initial capital is deposited and the paperwork submitted to the Ministry of Justice (*Hōmushō*).

When the permit is approved, congratulations, the *kaisha* is official. But then please don't forget to register your business with the Tax Office (*Zeimusho*).

To register the legal documents, a Japanese *inkan* (seal) is used to formally confirm a promoter's intent and responsibility. After the company is established, the same *inkan* must be used for business transactions with clients. Official documents to which the seal is applied are taken to the local government administrative office for certification that the seal is registered. Even foreigners cannot neglect these matters. Once a foreign resident with a specific address has completed foreign registration, it would be a good idea to make a personal official *inkan* seal.

G o o d *to* **k n o w** ·····································

●かいしゃをおこす [*kaisha o okosu*]	▷ found a company
●かぶしき [*kabushiki*]	▷ stock
●ほっきにん [*hokkinin*]	▷ originator, proposer, founder
●かぶしきがいしゃ [*kabushiki-gaisha*]	▷ joint stock company
●ゆうげんがいしゃ [*yūgen-gaisha*]	▷ limited-liability company
●ほうじん [*hōjin*]	▷ corporate body
●いんかんしょうめいしょ [*inkan shōmei-sho*]	▷ seal registration certificate

Section *3*

Basic Guide to Japanese Industries

The Software Industry

Growth expected

Japan's software industry centers around the custom development of software for the specialized needs of business enterprises and other organizations. In recent years, sales have increased with growing investments in information technology made both by private enterprises and by government agencies. The industry should see continued stable growth.

Japan's late start

The world's first computer was developed in the United States in 1946. But it was not until ten years later in 1956 that a computer was successfully developed in Japan.

In the beginning, Japanese computer makers had to compete for domestic market share with IBM, which already had worldwide competitive strength. One reason Japan lagged behind in developing software was the linguistic hurdle, i.e., the problem of adapting software to the special characteristics of the Japanese language. But even when Japanese-language software was successfully developed, its market was limited almost entirely to Japan.

Thus the development of Japanese software has centered around custom-made applications for domestic companies and other organizations instead of packaged software for global applications.

At the start of the 1990s, the software industry expanded significantly, supported by the large investments needed to bring financial institutions online.

But the end with the bursting of the economic, orders for custom software quickly dried up, making the mid-1990s a period of restructuring and personnel cuts for the industry.

Expanding IT-related investments

In recent years, the Internet brought advances in information technology (IT) and the IT revolution brought the rapid expansion of information-related investments by private firms and government agencies. Most companies outsource development of their software to development firms. So development of customized software for special management and information systems is a rapidly expanding industry.

Japan's central and local government agencies are digitalizing their paperwork. Many administrative services can now be done over the Internet, and there's growing acceptance of the concept of electronic government services. So Japanese software firms are now busy developing and marketing specialized software systems and security technology for this giant market.

Application service providers (ASP) have garnered a great deal of attention recently. These companies specialize in renting out relatively expensive applications via the Internet for contracted periods of time. This is advantageous for relatively small software companies since they do not need extensive resources to find and provide useful services to clients in this way.

So-called Internet data centers (IDCs) are also attracting considerable interest. These are large firms that specialize in supporting the customer's Internet business totally, with navigating services, security, storage, consulting and so on.

In the future, Japan's software industry will be partially supported by large government orders. But it will need to keep improving its development methods if it is to eliminate the technological lags that affected it in the past.

Growth trends in the software industry

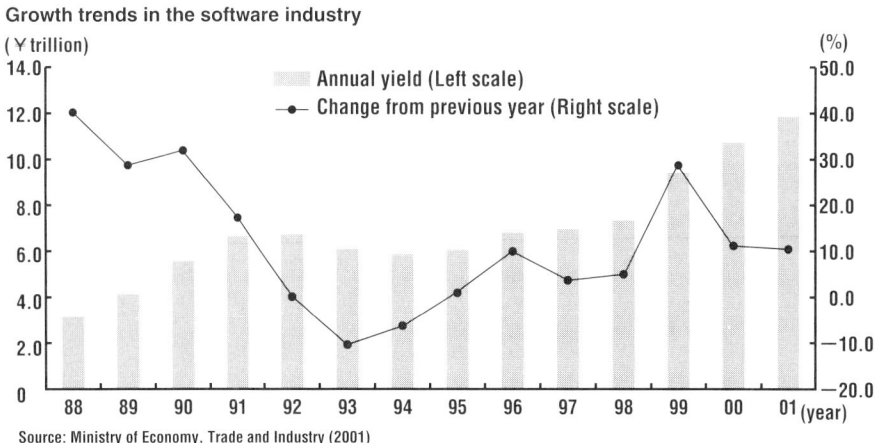

Source: Ministry of Economy, Trade and Industry (2001)

The Household Appliance Industry

Digitalization a key?

Personal expenditures for household electrical appliances hit a low point in the late 1990s, but in 2000 they exceeded the previous year for the first time in nine years. This trend toward recovery is expected to continue, and those in the industry think the key to further recovery will be the incorporation of digital controls and other devices in new-generation appliances.

Traditional patterns

In the electrical and machine industries, a traditional pattern has been for giant enterprises like Hitachi, Matsushita, Toshiba, and Sony to incorporate a large number of business lines within a single company. Household appliances, then, would be only one of the many lines.

Traditionally, profits from one business category might be reinvested in another thought to have particularly good prospects. Recently, however, more attention is paid to making each business category profitable on its own. And some corporations are spinning off businesses that are no longer closely controlled by the parent. In addition, there is a trend toward incorporating appliance manufacturing operations as separate companies.

Traditional mainstay appliances such as air conditioners, refrigerators, washing machines, and color TVs saturate the domestic market, so explosive growth in sales cannot be expected. Replacement sales, however, do mean steady demand from year to year.

Obviously, any significant increase in demand for household appliances will not come from traditional items. Instead, digitalization is making it possible to design a new generation of appliances that are smaller and smarter. One example is high-resolution TV sets. Another is better-quality, energy-saving audio equipment like miniaturized MD players. Among the successful new added-value products that incorporate screens for visual images are DVD players with large memories and high-resolution TVs with antennas and tuners that can receive digital satellite signals.

IT technology comes home

A new category of digital appliances that includes personal computers, cellular telephones, and electronic game machines is achieving considerable market growth.

The miniaturization and lower costs achieved during the second half of the 1990s will help put an estimated six million new cellular telephones into service in 2001 alone. The total number in service then will be over 60 million, or about one cellular or mobile phone for every two people in Japan.

TV game machines have also become an enormous market. In 2000 and 2001, a flood of new products with sophisticated functions, such as 3D graphics and high-quality sound, were introduced to the market.

In 1995, the advent of Windows 95 stimulated a phenomenal expansion of the PC market. The market for PCs and accessories — Internet modems, liquid crystal displays, digital cameras, and upgraded software — will likely expand further as new models are miniaturized and improved. Windows 98 and 2000 made the computer a communication tool through the Internet and Intranets. But nowadays, the cellular phone is going to take over part of that role.

Over the next ten years the demand for digital appliances should reach annual sales of 60 trillion yen. The key to business recovery in the household appliance industry will be to give special attention to digital appliances. However, sustained success will not be easy — partly because of the large investments needed for product development and the relatively short life-spans of popular products.

Good to know ···

Electronic industry production for consumer articles
(in comparison with the previous year)

	(thousand units)	(%)		(thousand units)	(%)
Color TVs	1,229	120.7	CD players	235	112.1
LCD TVs	73	168.1	MD players	299	99.7
VTRs	552	91.1	Car navigation systems	184	110.5
DVD video players	106	178.9	Car color TVs	75	116.2
Video cameras	131	81.5			

Source: Japan Electronics and Information Technology Industries Association, March 2001

Automobiles and Motorcycles

Global change in a key industry

The automotive sector of the economy is very large, employing over 10% of all Japanese wage-earners. It is also a very important industry for exports. At present, there is a market shift within Japan in favor of recreational vehicles and mini-cars. Recent years have brought major structural reforms to the automotive industry, both in Japan and overseas, but the degree of change now seems to be leveling off.

Worldwide restructuring

Isuzu, Suzuki, and Subaru are under the umbrella of General Motors; Mazda is under Ford; Nissan is under Renault; and Mitsubishi Motors under Daimler-Chrysler. Thus, there remain only two "purely Japanese" automotive concerns: Toyota and Honda.

At the end of the 20th century, the realignment of automakers leveled off, but in the 21st century we see new trend enveloping automotive parts makers. Nissan is selling off the majority of its shares in parts makers, and that will likely lead to speedy realignment in the former Nissan *keiretsu*.

To strengthen profitability, costs can be reduced by purchasing from parts makers

that are not necessarily of the same *keiretsu*. Automakers also use cooperative arrangements among themselves as a way of reducing the burdens of R&D, manufacturing, and sales. This sort of reorganization has made it possible for companies whose names were not well known abroad to strengthen recognition of their brands and to survive in the global marketplace.

Market changes

Significant changes have occurred in Japan's domestic market. Sales of traditional sedans have fallen off, while there has been an expansion in the market for minivans, station wagons and other so-called recreational vehicles. Market shares of standard passenger cars and small cars continue to decrease, but popularity of mini-cars is on the increase, especially among women. Mini-cars now account for one-third of the domestic automotive market.

Suzuki and Daihatsu have seen increases in sales due to the introduction of popular mini-vehicles.

As a result of the relocation of production facilities abroad and robust American and European economies, exports to North America, Europe, and Asia continue at a fairly high level.

New materials and electronic functions such as car navigation systems and electronic-control engines and transmissions are the key to increasing the value-added content of vehicles. Now aluminum is being used in the place of steel to make vehicles lighter and improve mileage.

Environmentally friendly vehicles

Consumers are becoming more aware of environmental issues, so automakers are hard at work developing new types of engines and fuels for economical, low-pollution vehicles. A good example is the hybrid car that operates with both a gasoline engine and an electric motor. The automakers that win consumers and survive in the future will likely be those that can develop innovative technology that doesn't harm the environment.

G o o d *to* k n o w ·

Japanese automobile production and vehicles exported   (Unit: No. of products)

	1999	2000 estimate	2001 forecast
Passenger cars	4,185,117	4,258,000	4,350,000
Standard cars	749,568	770,000	770,000
Small 4-wheel vehicles	2,160,083	2,233,000	2,350,000
Mini-cars (4-wheel)	1,275,466	1,255,000	1,230,000
Trucks (lorries)	1,681,008	1,706,000	1,735,000
Buses	15,866	16,000	15,000
Total for 4-wheel vehicles	5,881,991	5,980,000	6,100,000

Source: Japan Automobile Manufacturers Association, Inc.

The Petrochemical Industry

The restructuring of the largest enterprises

The petrochemical industry is the most important branch of Japan's overall chemical industry. And restructuring within this industry is taking place on a global scale. To survive, the largest Japanese enterprises are merging and otherwise reorganizing. A major point that bears watching is how well Japan can utilize its highly developed technology to make advances in global markets.

Petrochemical development and the pollution issue

Japan's post-war chemical industry developed largely around the production of chemical fertilizers. But in 1950, overproduction saturated the market and the industry went into decline.

Toward the end of the 1950s, however, petrochemicals brought great change to the character of Japan's chemical industry. A whole new array of products — ethylene being one of the most important — were manufactured and successfully marketed.

When the price of imported crude rose sharply in the 1970s as a result of the oil crises, Japan's petrochemical industry was deeply affected and its international competitive strength declined dramatically.

The Japanese government took these problems very seriously and encouraged the streamlining of plant operations and other structural reforms, with the result that the petrochemical industry recovered its profitability by the mid-1980s.

Along with the development of Japan's petrochemical and other chemical industries came the problem of pollution, which was brought to the public eye by the press.

Beginning in the 1970s, equipment was installed to mitigate the worst pollution problems and for some time everyone thought the problems were basically solved. However, in recent years new environmental issues related to the petro-chemical industry, such as dioxin or endocrine disrupters, have come to the fore, and the industry will no doubt have to shoulder more costly investments in preventative measures.

Japanese technology a key?

In the 21st century, Japan's petrochemical industry faces possible decline in international competitive strength due to the aging of its refineries and other manufacturing facilities.

In Asian countries other than Japan, for-eign-affiliated chemical makers have relatively new, large-scale plants, which produce a wide range of petrochemical products, and their sales are growing rapidly. Behind these developments are large American and European enterprises whose repeated and extensive restructuring greatly increased their productivity.

This caused Japan's petrochemical business to begin its own restructuring. To bolster their chances of survival,

many larger enterprises have merged or gone into cooperative agreements, have gotten rid of old facilities, and have built new and larger plants.

To compete with less expensive petro-chemical products from other countries, Japanese firms must utilize their highly developed technology to create distinctive and versatile products with substantial value-added features, high standards of quality, and a multiplicity of uses. For example, the combination of electronics and chemistry gave birth to technologies for microfabrication and thin films, which have spawned a wide array of new electronic components and materials.

Petrochemical companies should also expand their R&D activities into cutting-edge fields such as biotechnology, mixing advanced organic synthesis with genetic recombination, new materials, and electronic applications.

G o o d *to* k n o w ···

Trends in exports and imports of major petrochemical industrial products

(Unit: t)

Item	1999		2000	
	Export	Import	Export	Import
Ethylene	358,125	21,726	266,595	24,188
Propylene	496,486	1,213	396,315	3,025
Benzene	226,573	88,171	272,166	96,340
Toluene	15,375	45,550	10,907	127,873
Xylene	1,812,159	104,931	1,754,271	99,177

Source: Ministry of Finance

The Medical and Pharmaceutical Industries

The medical field in transition

With advancing research on genes and human genome, Japan's pharmaceutical industry entered a worldwide competition to develop new products that utilize genetic engineering. Also, more and more medically related enterprises are looking for business opportunities in the field of welfare, such as in-home care, in response to the new nursing-care insurance system that went into effect in April 2000.

Developing pharmaceuticals in a global market

Japan's market for pharmaceuticals is second only to that of the United States. However, the Japanese government has recently been trying to reduce its expenditures on prescription drugs to help limit ever-increasing medical costs. These limitations have kept the market from growing much in monetary terms.

Throughout the world, and especially in the United States, large enterprises quickly consolidated to join the race to develop new products that utilize genetic information from the deciphering of the human genome.

In Japan, the No.1 pharmaceutical manufacturer Takeda Chemical Industries announced that it acquired the rights to utilize the database of the human genome and gene information from Celera Genomics, a U.S. venture company that has already deciphered most of the human genome.

Looking toward global markets, overseas pharmaceutical firms are rapidly effecting mergers and other types of large-scale restructuring. Japanese pharmaceutical firms, too, are trying their best to develop new products for markets at home and abroad.

New pharmaceutical products require enormous investments, so pharmaceutical companies must place even more importance on R & D. No doubt Japanese pharmaceutical firms will also have to reorganize decisively through mergers and cooperative efforts. And unprofitable business lines will certainly be sold or discontinued.

Quite frankly, Japan is somewhat behind other countries in these new fields. However, new pharmaceutical products certainly offer many possibilities for Japan to recoup — depending, of course, on whether the industry can make the necessary drastic reforms.

The welfare industry in a graying society

Japan's society has one of the world's highest proportions of elderly people, creating a continuing need to improve nursing care and other welfare services. Nursing-care services for the elderly and preventative medicine are rapidly growing fields that anticipate these future needs.

Large medical-care organizations are starting up new businesses in response to the nursing-care insurance system that began in April 2000. Also, an increasing number of relatively small private enterprises now offer in-home services for the elderly. In fact, an April 2000 survey places the number of these small enterprises at around 34,000. They mainly offer nursing-care visits and rental of nursing-care and special-needs equipment.

However, there is a good deal of discontent about the low pay for nursing-care providers afforded by the nursing-care insurance system. This problem will surely affect the operation of these private service providers and the quality of the services they offer, if it is not remedied. To solve such problems, several groups of citizens' ombudsmen were established to check the services in their cities or towns.

All in all, nursing-care for the elderly is a field that is still under development, faced with tremendous problems. By the same token, it is a field that may develop into one of Japan's basic industries.

Preventative medicine and health care

In the future, much growth is expected in the realm of preventative medicine for chronic diseases such heart ailments, arterial sclerosis, diabetes, and some kinds of allergies.

In addition, with the increase in consumer demand for health care, bulk vitamins, calcium, and other kinds of supplements, as well as many kinds of cold remedies and gastrointestinal medicines, are sold over the counter.

 **G o o d** *to* **k n o w** ·

Production and value of medical drugs (Units: ¥ million, %)

Year	Total			Ethical drugs			OTC drugs and quasi-drugs		
	Value	Change	Ratio	Value	Change	Ratio	Value	Change	Ratio
1997	6,147,833	0.8	100.0	5,187,140	0.6	84.5	892,147	1.6	14.5
1998	5,842,096	−5.0	100.0	4,936,520	−4.8	84.4	839,150	−5.9	14.4
1999	6,290,023	7.7	100.0	5,438,173	10.2	86.5	793,026	−5.5	12.6

Source: Ministry of Health, Labor and Welfare

The Textile Industry

Japanese textiles in a slow market

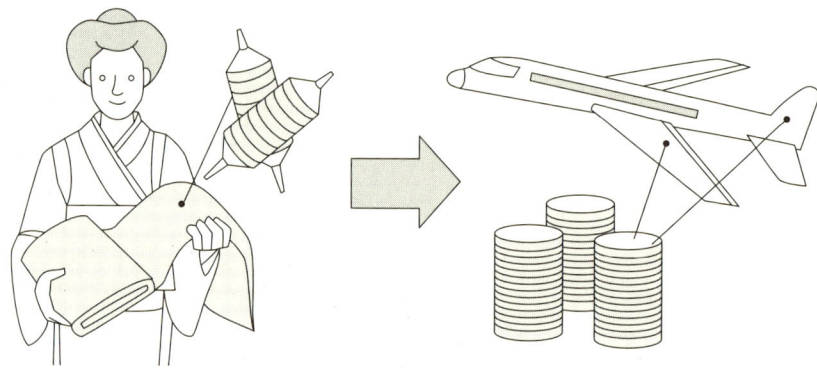

The textile industry was once an export mainstay that contributed greatly to Japan's economic development. In recent years, however, it has declined in the face of inexpensive foreign imports. On the other hand, the paper and pulp industry is going through a reorganization of major companies while domestic demand is increasing. As a result, the industry is beginning to show stable growth patterns.

The development and decline of the textile industry

Japan's textile industry developed with government encouragement during the Meiji Era, when its main products were silk and cotton goods. During the global economic depression of the 1930s, demand for silk exports fell drastically. Then, during WWII, raw cotton was virtually unobtainable. After the war, however, the government assisted the textile industry as part of its policy of reviving basic industries.

With increases in Japanese consumer demand, textile production continued to grow, providing goods for both domestic and foreign markets. Production of syn-

thetic fibers based on petroleum, with the help of imported technology, helped to maintain this growth.

Due to international trade friction, voluntary restrictions on textile exports were initiated in 1971. The industry was also negatively affected by the 1973 oil crisis and by appreciation of the yen.

South Korea, Taiwan, China and other regions of Asia also became textile sellers in the global export market, and their inexpensive products rapidly won market share in Japan's domestic market as well, putting ever more pressure on the Japanese textile industry.

Diversification

To survive in the 21st century, the textile industry is developing new products aimed at helping it recover its former prosperity. Among them are carbon fibers, which are lighter and more flexible than traditional textiles, and show promise for use in aircraft parts and for construction and civil engineering projects.

Textile firms also make use of their scientific and technological expertise to diversify beyond textiles and fibers. Today their products include synthetic goods, medical supplies, foods, semiconductors, and materials for magnetic tapes.

Traditional synthetic fibers and fabrics have to compete with inexpensive imports, so the manufacturers are developing high value-added fibers and fabrics. If they are to maintain domestic market shares and make inroads abroad, these manufacturers will have to make full use of Japan's technological prowess in the development of new products.

The paper industry

Japan is the second largest producer of pulp for paper after the United States. The U.S. supplies 30 percent of the global demand, while Japan supplies 10 percent. Japan imports newsprint and printing paper from Europe and the U.S., but this accounts for only about four percent of the domestic market, a figure much lower than in most other countries. Just as in the fiber industry, this is because of the different tastes between Japan and the West.

Production of pulp requires large facilities, and a past race among competitors to invest in facilities resulted in surplus production capacity, which weakened the market. Large joint ventures were formed in 1993 and 1996. And then Nippon Unipac Holding was established on March 30, 2001 by the integration of Nippon Paper Industries (No.2) and Daishowa Paper Mfg. (No.4). It will surely become the leading pulp company in Japan by responding to globalization and meeting consumer needs.

G o o d *to* k n o w ·····································

Performance of Japan's big eight fiber manufacturers

(Fiscal year ending March 2000, consolidated basis; Unit:100-million yen)

Companies	Yield	Profit	Ratio of profit from fibers	Companies	Yield	Profit	Ratio of profit from fibers
Asahi Kagaku Kogyo Co., Ltd.	11,945	859	12%	Kuraray Co., Ltd.	3,164	221	31%
Toray Industries, Inc.	9,905	249	41%	Kanebo, Ltd.	5,684	192	30%
Teijin Ltd.	6,042	202	53%	Mitsubishi Rayon Co., Ltd.	3,139	169	33%
Toyobo Co., Ltd.	4,149	76	56%	Unitika Ltd.	2,931	76	47%

Source: 「業界のしくみ」PHP研究所

Steel and Nonferrous Metals

From quantity to quality

Good!

Japan's steel industry is operating in an ever-more-exacting environment. Steel companies want to move away from mere mass production of bulk steel and concentrate on specialty and high-quality steel products. They are also looking for more versatile management styles that will stimulate engineering businesses with high growth potential. The nonferrous industry, which includes aluminum, copper, and other such metals, is also struggling to survive by focusing on products for emerging high-tech industries.

A mature steel industry

Japan's steel industry was able to expand globally because its plants and ports on the Pacific Rim made it cost-effective to ship products around the world. In fact, it's still cheaper to ship steel from Tokyo to Los Angeles than from Chicago to Los Angeles.

Also, Japan's production of pig iron has long been number one in the world. However, overproduction of certain products resulted in wholesale price-cutting, which was exacerbated by increasing steel production in other Asian countries. Thus Japan's steel industry left the growth stage and became a mature industry in which growth and even survival could no longer be taken for granted.

To cope with the new environment, steel companies are forming new strategic partnerships. For example, in early 2000 Japan's second and third ranking steelmakers, Nippon Kokan (NKK) and Kawasaki Steel, entered into a broad cooperative arrangement with an eye to a future merger with National Steel in U.S.A. and Thyssen in Germany. And in August 2000 the world's second-largest steelmaker, Nippon Steel, concluded a strategic partnership with POSCO, the steelmaker giant in South Korea. Other strategic partnerships of global significance are in the works, fueled by efforts of Japanese steelmakers to maintain competitive strength at home and abroad.

Japan's outstanding strengths in technology

The Japanese steel industry's successful response to the many-faceted needs of the domestic market led to unsurpassed technological strengths. High-quality composite materials — e.g., high-tensile steel sheets that help reduce automobile body weight and steel panels designed to prevent vibrations in washing machines — are highly acclaimed in global markets.

The industry's computer-aided manufacturing processes and energy-saving technologies for heat reutilization are on the cutting edge. Steel companies hope to return to profitability through further restructuring, greater rationalization of manufacturing processes, and realization of inter-factory cooperative agreements. However, as of the beginning of the 21st century, the business environment is still difficult and the key strategic concepts are wide-ranging business partnerships, and concentration of resources and technologies.

High-profit nonferrous products

Manufacturers of aluminum, copper, and other nonferrous metals have made significant inroads into the production of silicon-based products, optical fibers, and other electronic materials. Mitsui Mining and Smelting has brisk markets for the electronic parts known as TAB, which are used for assembling liquid crystal screens, and also for copper-foil parts for portable telephones. Mitsubishi Materials has found a niche in silicon wafer manufacture, while Sumitomo Metals & Mining has invested a great deal of effort in optical communications. Because IT-related demand is expected to increase, nonferrous metal companies should prosper over the coming years.

In addition to information technology, other promising high-profit fields include insulated aluminum door and window frames and solar batteries.

Semi-processed nonferrous metals are considered international commodities, and their prices are influenced greatly by currency exchange rates and by transactions on the London Metal Exchange (LME). Nonferrous metal refineries saw their profits drop in the first quarter of fiscal 2000, for instance, because of an appreciating yen.

G o o d *to* **k n o w** ·

Iron and steel production, exports and imports (Unit:1,000t)

	1996	1997	1998	1999	2000
Production Crude steel	98,801	104,545	3,548	94,178	106,442
Production Ordinary steel products	77,974	81,927	73,183	73,145	87,565
Exports (iron and steel)	20,615	23,501	27,649	28,212	29,159
Imports (iron and steel)	8,625	9,569	6,631	6,472	7,747

Source: Japan Iron and Steel Federation

The Machine Industry

Robots making robots

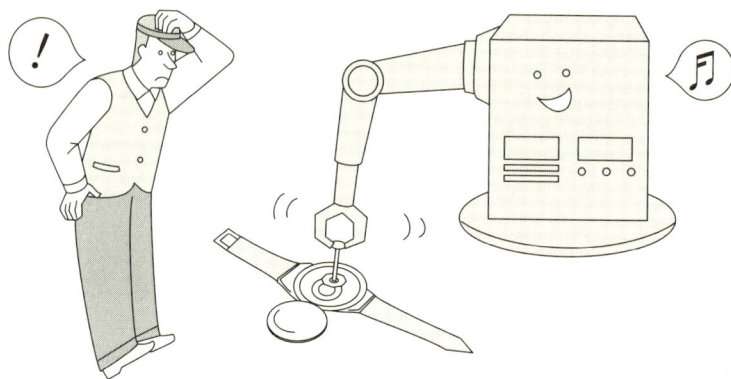

Japan makes over half the world's robots used in manufacturing processes. About half of these industrial-use robots are exported. So it's no exaggeration to say that Japanese robots are playing vital roles in the manufacture of various types of machines throughout the world. Recently much attention is being given to the humanoid robot made by the Honda Motor Co. called ASIMO, which walks on two legs. The age of robots making robots is at hand.

Electronic control technology

Japan has developed outstanding technologies for the electronic control of machines, and this has helped the country maintain its international competitive strength in the field of machine tools. During the 1970s and 1980s, increasing quantities of relatively inexpensive, highly functional Japanese machine tools that made use of sophisticated electronic control technology were exported to other countries. This gave rise to considerable trade friction. This caused Japanese machine tool manufacturers to build production facilities in America and Europe and to further globalize their operations by procuring a large proportion of their parts and materials from other countries in Asia.

After the collapse of Japan's bubble economy, domestic demand for sophisticated machine tools fell because the recession caused a decline in investments in plants and facilities. To survive, companies in this field started rationalization programs, and began putting emphasis on improved precision and functionality as well as on new systems for coordinating the operations of machines of different types or in different locations.

Accepting new challenges

One noteworthy fact of recent years is that, in spite of Japan's long business recession, new machines that use advanced technologies continue to appear and find customers. Among these are super-high-speed machines with linear motors.

What's new in the field of measuring devices, Japanese technology continues to surprise the world, and some of the newest high-precision devices can accurately measure at nanometer (one-millionth of a millimeter) levels.

Advances in such technologies as actuators and sensors, together with new developments in artificial intelligence, mean that some of Japan's leading-edge robots can closely approximate human movement and use fuzzy logic programming to approximate human behavior. Besides industrial robots, some of Japan's newest robots are also pets.

New wave of precision machines

Watches and other timepieces have been developed with sophisticated value-added functions related to communications. Digital cameras that can communicate with personal computers are fast replacing film cameras, and nearly all Japanese camera manufacturers have quit making products strictly for film and

are making a transition to electronic products.

Makers of precision machines are diversifying, giving a good deal of attention, for example, to semiconductor-related products.

Technologies for protecting the environment

In keeping with the responsibilities of an industrially advanced nation, Japan's machine industry is using state-of-the-art technology to further diversify and develop equipment and processes that help prevent pollution and protect the environment. Some of their products include devices for trash incinerators that minimize carbon dioxide emissions and such atmospheric pollutants as nitrogen oxides and sulfur oxides. Others address a worldwide need for equipment to prevent water pollution during the treatment of liquid industrial wastes, sewage, and human wastes. They have been so successful so far that great expectations have arisen. And many expect Japan's versatile machine industry can surely make major contributions in the field of environmental protection.

G o o d *to* **k n o w** ·

Precision equipment shipments (1999)   (Unit: ¥ million)

Medical machinery and devices	548,591	35 mm cameras	160,436
Scales and other measuring devices	311,765	Optical lenses	128,119
Watches and clocks	196,955	Watch and clock parts	118,782

Source: Ministry of Economy, Trade and Industry

Food and Agricultural Products

Getting out of a slump

The food industry has had to respond to the growing variety of Japanese eating habits. Safety and high quality are two keys. Lack of young farm workers and competition with cheap imported produce are the serious issues that must be resolved. Nevertheless, the agricultural industry will undoubtedly leave the current slump behind as productivity grows, thanks in part to a relaxation of government regulations.

Changes in consumer needs

Since the 1990s, per capita food consumption, as well as food prices, have declined. Food expenditure as a portion of family budgets continues to be relatively low. Also, continuing sharp competition among processed food products contributes to falling prices.

The fierce competition among food processors has had another salutory effect. These producers are now much more sensitive to consumer concerns, such as the public's increasing health consciousness.

In 2000, Snow Brand Milk Products, a large dairy products company, was responsible for widespread food poisoning. In the ensuing investigation, other food processors were also found to have

marketed adulterated products. This caused consumers to become more cautious, which contributed to the overall slump in the food products market.

Competing for market shares

Unlike some other industries, the food industry operates within a natural limit of demand. Thus battles for shares of this limited market are inevitable and it becomes very difficult for food processors and distributors to survive. Effective marketing is essential, and that means continual collection of detailed data on consumer wants and needs.

Recent examples of marketing success include the several brands of a low-malt beer-like beverage that is less expensive than ordinary beer. In February 2001, consumer demand forced Asahi Breweries to join its pioneering competitors in marketing this type of beverage.

Low-calorie foods and red wine sell briskly because of the growing health awareness of consumers.

Where food safety is concerned, the lesson in the repeated incidents of food poisoning is that food producers and processors must pay close attention to product safety to gain consumer confidence. Organic vegetables grown without pesticides are expected to gain higher sales, because of consumer health concerns.

Rice and market principles

Japan's agricultural products — especially rice, the staple food — were the long protected from foreign imports by government.

After passage of the new Foodstuff Control Law in 1995, government regulations were eased and market principles introduced. The idea was: (1) to adjust the balance of the demand and supply of rice, (2) to fix prices depending on the market, and (3) to make Japanese rice more competitive with imports, which were partially allowed as a result of the GATT Uruguay Round agricultural agreement of 1994.

Regulations now permit agricultural entrepreneurs to incorporate their operations as companies. They also allow retailers/distributors to newly enter this market from different lines of business.

Battle for survival

Japan is one of the world's largest importers of farm products. The self-sufficiency rate for rice was about 90% at the end of the 20th century, but that of vegetables was only 40%, even though it was 100% up to about 1965. The rate for soybeans, essential to the Japanese diet, is a mere 3%. With even cheaper imports now coming to Japan from China, the battle of survival for Japanese farmers is likely to heat up further.

In April 2001, Japan invoked safeguards on three Chinese agricultural products: leeks, *shiitake* mushrooms, and rushes for *tatami* matting. The trade restrictions are used as temporary measures, but it is important for both the government and farmers to develop more innovative, long-range plans to help Japanese farmers survive.

G o o d *to* k n o w •

Volume and value of major farm imports (2000) (¥ : 100 million)

	Category	Value	Change from 1999		Category	Value	Change from 1999
	Farm products	39,714	−3.0%				
1	Soybeans	1,319	−5.3%	4	Pork	3,475	6.7%
2	Wheat	1,111	−9.1%	5	Fresh vegetables	1,018	−3.6%
3	Beef	2,799	0.3%	6	Frozen vegetables	891	−7.1%

Source: Ministry of Agriculture, Forestry and Fisheries

Banking and Securities

A disproven myth

In Japan, there was once the myth that banks cannot fail. But in 1992, an Osaka Credit Union went bankrupt, followed by two Tokyo credit banks and other financial institutions in 1994. Today, Japan's banking and securities industries are going through a period of rapid change with restructuring and partnerships reaching beyond traditional boundaries.

The birth of new financial groups

The financial system experienced a new spate of instability with the failures of the Hokkaido Takushoku Bank and Yamaichi Securities in 1997. Although public funds were pumped into financial institutions, it failed to resolve their bad debt problems. The financial world went on the defensive as more large financial institutions failed; then some of the larger banks launched aggressive moves to deal with the situation.

Beginning with the Mizuho Financial Group (Dai-Ichi Kangyo Bank, Industrial Bank of Japan, and Fuji Bank) in September 2000, and the merger of Sumitomo Bank and Sakura Bank to form SMBC in April 2001, four giant banking groups were formed within one year. This stimulated other reorganizations such as the formation of comprehensive financial groups that go beyond traditional boundaries to include securities and life and accident insurance companies.

These changes were facilitated by looser government regulations. For example, investment trusts (*tōshi shintaku*) can now be handled by banks, while in the past only specialized securities firms and trust companies could provide them. Since early 2001, banks can sell insurance as well as a wide variety of financial products.

New banking businesses

There are now four basic types of banks: (1) the Big Four, which compete globally with foreign financial groups; (2) smaller banks concerned mainly with domestic retail business; (3) firms specializing in investments, trusts, and so forth; and (4) Internet banks that have no brick-and-mortar branches but conduct banking business strictly in cyberspace. The latter two types, are open to participation by businesses other than traditional banks.

In addition, overseas groups with sophisticated financial know-how are also finding niches. A key to survival for the Japanese banks will be innovative management to increase competitiveness, after coping with the remaining burdens of bad debt.

The growth of the Internet securities business

The old securities industry structure that had smaller firms operating under the umbrella of four giant securities companies (with Nomura Securities at the top) has changed. In the future, it will probably center on the four newly organized financial groups mentioned above. Nomura, Daiwa, and other large security firms weathered the lingering stock market doldrums by making huge cuts in costs, improving services to companies, and diversifying their sources of income. In addition, deregulation now permits securities transactions to be conducted over the Internet. Internet securities businesses can charge less for their services, so their market share is rapidly growing.

These seismic changes in the financial and securities industries are sometimes referred to as the Financial Big Bang, borrowing a phrase from Britain. Companies are shifting from indirect to direct financing. And the opening of the Nasdaq exchange adds new financing opportunities for these businesses, as does the influx of money from individual investors using the Internet.

Good to know

Bad debt held by private-sector financial institutions (Unit: ¥ trillion)

	Savings	Bad debt
Large banks	349.8	40.9
Regional second-level banks	186.0	22.5
Trusts, unions, coops, and others	137.6	18.4
Total	673.3	81.7

Source: Financial Services Agency, end of March 2000

Wholesaling and Retailing

The fight for survival

Convenience stores and other chainstores prospered in 1990s. Now, however, strong companies that can acquire good retail locations are expanding the number of their stores, and competition is becoming more severe. More traditional and longer-established retailers are under a lot of pressure. Major restructuring is taking place among department stores and in the supermarket industry, which has leveled off despite the burgeoning convenience stores.

Strong convenience stores

Retailing in general has found it difficult to recover from the long economic slump of the 1990s. Convenience stores, however, were the exception. In February 2001, Seven-Eleven Japan surpassed Daiei's sales to become Japan's largest retailer. In contrast, No.2 retailer Daiei, the major general merchandise chain, made a series of restructuring efforts, but they did not bring the expected results.

Convenience stores have designed innovative information systems, and they stock their limited store space only with products proven to sell briskly. Today, their information systems have gone far beyond retail to facilitate payment of electricity and telephone bills, and even as points of contact for nursing-care services and Internet stock transactions.

The convenience store chains have excellent store-management know-how, which has led to many requests, especially from China, Korea, and other Asian countries, for overseas expansion. The Family Mart and Mini Stop chains have set up operations in Korea, and the Lawson chain has entered China.

Because Japan's convenience stores have gone beyond retailing to provide financial and other services needed by society, for the moment, at least, they should see continued growth.

An uncertain future for department stores

Department stores, most of which have long histories, are the traditional retail industry leaders, but they have found it hard to maintain sales levels. In fact, Sogo department stores applied for protection from creditors through the Corporate Rehabilitation Law in July 2000.

In trying to cope with the long slump in consumer spending, department stores have begun to sell cheaper brands of apparel, and to rent parts of their floor space to popular brand-name boutiques. In addition, many department stores have redecorated their basement food floor, one of the most attractive sections for their customers, to meet strong demands for prepared food, confections, and other high-class foods.

Department stores are struggling to create new customer appeal, no longer being able to rely solely on customer trust built up over the years to survive the retail wars of the 21st century.

Advances by specialty chainstores

One retail chain making rapid advances is named Fast Retailing. It added 38 stores in 2000 and doubled profits in a single year. Its inexpensive but high-quality casual wear brand is UNIQLO, which is a coined word that is part *uniq*ue and part *clo*thing(warehouse).

Another recent development is discount stores, many offering merchandise at half or even 80 or 90 percent off the normal retail price. And the everything-for-100-yen shops are perennial favorites. Direct volume purchasing from the manufacturers make these deep discounts possible. Money goes directly from the store to the manufacturer, doing away with the middleman, warehousing, and other distribution costs.

Good to know ···

Number of retail stores by category, annual sales

(Unit: ¥ trillion)

	No. of outlets	Annual sales
Retail businesses (total)	1,419,685	147.7541
Department stores	480	10.6860
Consolidated supermarkets	1,886	9.9475
Specialized supermarkets	32,208	20.4401
Convenience stores	36,586	5.2197
Other supermarkets	120,577	9.9783
Specialty outlets	839,966	59.6890
Quasi-specialty outlets	385,928	31.5401
Other retail outlets	2,054	0.2535

Source: Ministry of Economy, Trade and Industry, Census of Commerce 1997

General Trading Companies

The end of an era?

Mitsubishi Corporation, Marubeni, and many other large trading companies (called *sōgō shōsha*) did much to help Japan's economic prosperity in the post-war period. However, in recent years their business patterns have changed in fundamental ways. The very traditional raison d'être of the *sōgō shōsha* is being called into question as Japanese manufacturers more frequently import raw materials and export their own products rather than go through trading companies. Organizationally, the *sōgō shōsha* have undergone many splits and mergers, and have started new businesses that are completely different from their traditional activities.

Sōgō Shōsha

The *shōsha* were basically middlemen handling the import of metals, fibers and textiles, foods, oil and natural gas, building materials, and a great variety of sophisticated manufactured imports like machinery or even missiles for the Self Defense Forces. Together, Japan's *shōsha* handle more than 100 trillion yen in imports annually, or some 20% of Japan's gross national product (GNP).

The largest, most diversified, and best-known trading companies are known as *sōgō shōsha*, or general trading companies. These *sōgō shōsha* are well known internationally for their distinctive organizations, and for their long-continued business growth.

They have also traditionally served as business organizers, especially abroad, and as mid-term financial institutions. In recent years, however, these firms have undergone great changes. In fact, the trading companies have passed the peak of their import activities as their main traditional customers among Japanese manufacturers and retailers have turned increasingly to direct dealings with overseas providers.

In the years of Japan's bubble economy, *sōgō shōsha* made large investments in other Asian countries and in Japanese real estate. After the economic bubble burst, real estate prices plummeted and the *sōgō shōsha* lost huge sums of money.

Opening new lines of business

Today the *sōgō shōsha* are worried that their traditional role as middlemen may become even less important. So they are developing new businesses to supplement their traditional activities.

The multimedia activities of *sōgō shōsha* are particularly noticeable. For example, they have opened virtual malls on the Internet, and are getting into cable TV and digital satellite broadcasting services.

They are also advancing into the financial field. With the extensive relaxation of government regulations on financial markets, the *sōgō shōsha* hope to become new financial institutions of global importance.

The *sōgō shōsha* own strong capital positions in Japan's convenience store chains. The *sōgō shōsha* hope to utilize the convenience stores' well-developed digital networks, which are closely linked to consumers in their neighborhoods, as sales points for their new communications and financial services.

Sōgō shōsha are putting large sums of money into IT ventures and making overseas investments such as in the Indonesian petrochemical industry, so it would seem that they are now more concerned with investments than with their traditional role as middlemen and traders.

In their traditional trading role, the *sōgō shōsha* are nevertheless trying to differentiate themselves from other goods distributors by emphasizing quality rather than quantity, and by trying create ate distinctive added value.

If the *sōgō shōsha* can manage their large burdens of debt, and if they can rebuild their identities to encompass new high-growth businesses — including new ways and means to work as middlemen and traders — then we may see new kinds of Japanese *sōgō shōsha* in the 21st century.

Good to know ·

Sales of eight general trading companies (FY1999) (Unit: ¥ million)

Company	Sales	Company	Sales
Mitsui & Co., Ltd.	13,200,716	Marubeni Corp.	10,222,442
Mitsubishi Corp.	13,109,117	Nissho Iwai Corp.	7,281,304
Itochu Corp.	12,144,445	Tomen Corp.	2,866,909
Sumitomo Corp.	10,672,407	Nichimen Corp.	2,861,907
		Total	72,359,247

Source: Ministry of Economy, Trade and Industry

Construction and Housing

A difficult future?

In the near future, the construction industry will likely be affected by cuts in the public spending on which this industry has greatly depended, and new housing starts are expected to decrease. To prosper, Japan's construction and housing industries must find ways to promote new added value.

Types and reasons for restructuring

General contractors (usually abbreviated as *gene-con*) have traditionally received orders for construction projects and then subcontracted out much of the actual work. During the bubble economy, the giant general contractors incurred huge debts, which led to bankruptcy or near insolvency for many of them in the late 1990s and early 21st century.

Large private land development declined in the post-bubble years, and there will likely be fewer public works projects, although they were once considered an important boost to the economy in times of recession. As a result,

investment in construction lags. As the situation now stands, the nearly 700,000 construction and construction-related companies (mostly subcontractors) are just too many. Competition for new orders keeps getting more severe, and bid prices for private construction projects continue to fall.

These difficulties seem to be causing changes in the multi-layered structure of subcontractors. To lower costs, bids are being taken from outside the traditional families of construction companies. And some subcontractors are starting to bypass the general contractors entirely, seeking orders directly from clients.

One hopeful sign in the construction industry is the incorporation of value-added, intelligent, IT-ready buildings. After the Great Hanshin-Awaji Earthquake of 1995, the industry made new efforts to develop the technology necessary to ensure the safety and seismic durability of the structures they build. But in the severe environment now surrounding the construction industry, only those that provide added value, develop viable and appropriate technology, have strong financial footing, and bring in pertinent technology from outside the company will survive.

Fewer new residences?

In 1999, new housing starts numbered 1.22 million. However, the declining birth rate and increasing housing availability and durability will likely reduce new housing starts to about 1 million by 2010. Thus, homebuilders are becoming more interested in pre-owned homes and in remodeling.

In Japan's housing industry, the market share held by the largest companies is lower than might be supposed. The 10 largest homebuilders account for only about 30% of the market. The remaining 70% belongs to relatively small local companies.

Some of the big companies plan to expand their market shares as a means of coping with the coming decline in housing starts. One new field homebuilders have developed is post-construction installation of IT devices. Many new apartments have standard Internet access capabilities, and other uses of IT devices include shopping, home security, medical care, and leisure.

In April 2000, a law promoting housing quality went into effect. This will cause greater competition to provide better quality, so the companies that survive will be those that offer trustworthy, long-term post-construction maintenance services.

G o o d *to* **k n o w** ·······························

Number of new housing starts in 2000

(Unit: homes) (%)

District	Total number	Ratio to previous year
Hokkaido	49,876	−3.5
Tohoku	77,039	−6.7
Kanto	484,428	1.9
Hokuriku	42,752	−3.9
Chubu	147,804	0.1

District	Total number	Ratio to previous year
Kinki	192,852	−4.9
Chugoku	60,751	−2.4
Shikoku	32,487	−3.1
Kyushu	112,476	−0.7
Okinawa	12,692	1.4

Source: Ministry of Land, Infrastructure and Transportation

The Transportation Industry

Fiercer competition for service

Japan's transportation industry supports the country's economy in many ways, and it plays a tremendous role. One key to the future will be more efficient ways of distributing goods, especially in direct response to consumer needs. And now that government regulation of airlines has been relaxed, a key to their future growth will be cheaper, more innovative, larger-volume airline ticket sales.

Changes in transportation

Japan's first railroad opened in 1872, running between Tokyo's Shimbashi Station and Yokohama. Railroad networks then rapidly spread across the country, and for many years they were the principal means for the long-distance transport of passengers and goods.

In the 1960s, many roads were paved and railroads were joined by cars and trucks as principal means of transportation. Japan's major expressways such as the Shuto, Tomei, and Meishin were completed in the 1960s.

Airplane travel in the postwar period developed rather slowly because Japanese travel abroad was severely restricted, until the government removed the embargo on overseas sightseeing tours in 1964. With the coming of jumbo jets and in the economic boom in the 1970s, domestic air transportation demand rapidly increased, and new airports were built to serve Japan's larger cities.

At present, the earnings of Japan's JR railway lines — which were once publicly owned — are rather flat because many people choose to travel by automobile and airplane. However, the JR railways are offering campaigns and fare discounts in an effort to be more competitive. The non-JR private railways also saw declining business following the collapse of the bubble economy. And both

JR and other private railways have shut down many unprofitable local lines in rural areas.

Government regulation of airlines was relaxed in February 2000 and domestic fares were completely deregulated. Also, more severe price competition among domestic airlines resulted from the appearance of new companies like Air Do, which offers low-price flights between Tokyo and Sapporo.

Better service on the way?

Overall improvement in economic conditions during 2000 helped the railways industry recover to some degree from its long business slump. Nevertheless, Japan's declining birth rate and the graying of its society are expected to gradually reduce the number of people commuting to work and school. In other words, any spectacular business growth for railways in the future is unlikely.

One survival strategy in this age of multiple transport competition for the railways is to improve train stations and the surroundings.

JR firms were established with the split-up of Japanese National Railways in 1987, and they have tried to take drastic restructuring measures. In February 2001, the government sold all its stock in East Japan, West Japan, and Tokai JR lines. The move completed the privatization of the three JR groups.

Immediately after the deregulation of domestic airfares, carriers began offering discount air tickets. Internet systems through which users can reserve and purchase air tickets directly, without going through travel agents, has lowered prices and helped customers find the information they need.

And finally, a little about transportation vehicles. Diesel trucking firms will likely experience some difficulties because Tokyo Metropolitan Government announced that it is going to forbid trucks with diesel engines from entering the city. These regulations will not directly force the makers to do anything, but they will surely cause them to consider the effect of their products on the environment and people's health.

Door-to-door delivery service

The business of door-to-door delivery service, called *Takuhaibin* has enjoyed continuing growth these twenty years. Yamato, the leading company of home delivery service, has created various services to satisfy customer needs, such as time period delivery service, which enables customer to choose the delivery time from six possible delivery times.

Recently, motorcycles and bicycles are being used very profitably for short-distance deliveries at the urban areas. Here, too, the key is how well these services can respond to customer needs.

The Communications Industry

The fiercest competition of all …

Even more than with the rest of Japan's economy, the communications industry has been engulfed in great changes over the last several years. As a result, it has now entered an age of extremely sharp competition. Companies have effected mergers and cooperative agreements and introduced new services one after the other in their continuing struggle for greater shares of the market.

Big changes in business structure

Influenced by deregulation and burgeoning technological innovations, the communications industry finds it must cope with a highly sophisticated information society and then an even more sophisticated one in the next generation. Of course, this causes the major players in the industry to restructure, often more than once.

In negotiations concerning government deregulation in the year 2000, the United States asked for lower hook-up fees from NTT (the largest player in Japan's communications industry). In fact, it became a major issue. Although this dispute was later put on the back burner, new problems with NTT's business organization have emerged, and now the U.S. demands further restructuring.

Some of the more important changes in the industry related to mobile or cellular telephones, with the coming of handsets that have both voice and data communications capabilities. To be able to connect with the Internet through a cellular telephone is a welcome development for the younger generation as well as for almost everyone in business. In 2001, the i-mode cellular telephone marketed by NTT DoCoMo was especially popular. The fierce battle for market share will surely continue.

In the area of communications infrastructure, scientists are working on still faster and higher-capacity circuitry, and new services utilizing broad-band capacity ADSL, optical fibers, and cable television continue to appear. In these fields, too, the competition is heating up. Actually, Bluetooth wireless technology may be more important than faster circuits, at least to consumers. NTT trunk lines are rapidly introducing optical fiber to the home, and competitors like KDDI are working on them, too.

A still higher-information society?

Triggered by NTT's restructuring, several new entities have become industry players. First of all, the Japan Telecom group has amalgamated several other domestic communications firms and this new Japan Telecom-based company — the third largest in the field — has increased its capital resources through cooperative arrangements with Britain's Vodafone Group so as to better challenge the predominant position of NTT.

In October 2000, KDD, DDI, and IDO merged to become KDDI, which is now Japan's second largest communications company. Keen competition among these three largest companies leading to lower hook-up costs is to be expected.

KDDI and the J-phone companies have developed Internet-access portable telephones, each with some special feature to compete with NTT's i-mode. A next-generation mobile telephone service capable of super-fast data communication, known as W-CDMA, appeared on the market in 2001. We shall have to wait and see how successful these products will be as composite data tools in such diverse areas as music, visual images, and personal information.

Main issues that will affect competition in the area of communications infrastructure are of course speed and high capacity, but perhaps most vital area of all will be the lowering of user fees.

G o o d *to* **k n o w** ·

Share by domestic mobile telephone providers

NTT DoCoMo (NTT group)	59.1%
au (KDDI group)	18.0%
J-PHONE (Japan Telecom group)	16.4%
TU-KA (KDDI group)	6.5%

End of March 2001

The Mass Communications Industry

The wave of digitalization

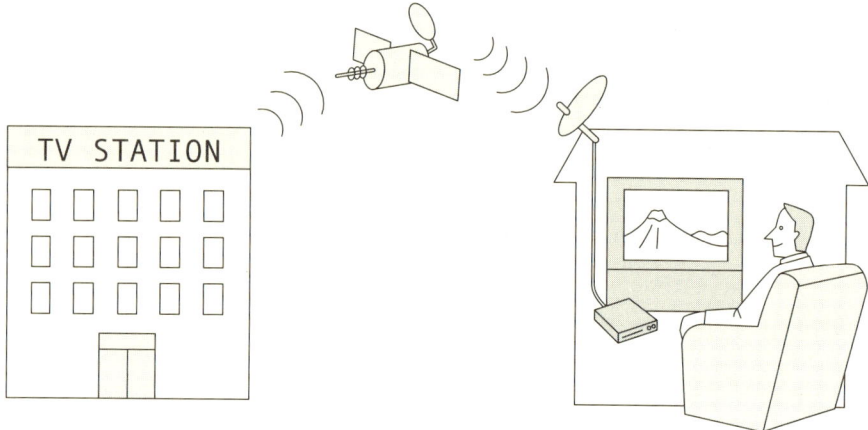

Traditionally, mass communications refers to conveying information to the public through the four major media: newspapers, magazines, TV, and radio. However, in recent years, mass media worldwide have had to respond to the digital revolution. Japan is no exception.

The development of Japan's mass communications

Japan's first daily newspaper, the Yokohama Mainichi Shimbun, began in 1870. As public interest in society grew and as printing technology progressed, print media emerged.

A large proportion of Japan's daily newspapers is directly delivered to subscribers rather than sold at newsstands. The largest-circulation newspaper, the Yomiuri, prints 10 million copies daily (morning and afternoon editions), and the Asahi prints 8 million copies. These are much larger numbers than those of influential dailies in other countries. The New York Times, for example, prints only about 1 million copies per day.

The broadcast industry began with the first radio broadcast service in 1925. NHK, or the Japan Broadcasting Corporation, was established in 1926. After the war, several private broadcasting companies arose and were able to provide information that responded to the public's needs. Television broadcasts began in 1953, and now there are five key networks. In 1984, BS broadcasting started. The total number of VHF/UHF TV stations (including NHK and University of the Air) was 128 in 2000.

Digitalization in the media

Newspapers, magazines, TV and radio are all being touched by a wave of digitalization, and Japan is changing as a result.

First of all, in the advertising world, Internet ads have spread rapidly, with the increase of Internet users. Not only banner ads, but also mail magazine ads, text-only ads, and others are now on the 'Net and are expected to grow. Thus, advertisers can go direct, and offer direct sales, without going through an advertising agency.

The digitalization of broadcasting is also progressing, with particular growth seen in multi-channel broadcasting.

Communication satellite broadcasting (CS) started in 1992, offering multi-channel services. But subscribers totaled only about 8 million in 1999. They are trying to increase subscribers by providing high-speed Internet services.

Broadcast satellite (BS) digital hi-resolution broadcasting began in December 2000, permitting upgraded picture quality, greater channel availability, and interactive services. The future looks good for this part of the broadcast industry.

Publication without printing?

The printing and publication industry, which has already had to adjust to a decline in readers, is being further challenged by the Internet. However, some new business opportunities are have arisen due to this digital trend. Large Japanese publishers like Kodansha, Shogakukan, and Shueisha are selling the content of their publications online via the Internet, and we also see various new strategies for attracting readers, such as online-shopping or providing information on recently published books.

As the mass communications industry is hit by this wave of digitalization, Japan is at the trial-and-error stage in its efforts to best utilize these new means for transmitting information.

G o o d *to* k n o w ....

Trend in national morning newspaper sales (Unit: No. of papers)

	Yomiuri	Asahi	Mainichi	Nikkei
1975	6,412,567	6,747,909	4,426,587	1,601,527
1980	8,486,772	7,506,263	4,639,855	1,823,629
1985	8,852,610	7,533,727	4,203,658	2,126,183
1990	9,805,480	8,191,226	4,190,744	2,911,454
1995	10,050,285	8,252,192	3,989,805	2,869,438
2000	10,224,066	8,322,046	3,976,357	3,044,214

Source: Japan Audit Bureau of Circulations

The Leisure Industry

Leisure and the IT revolution

 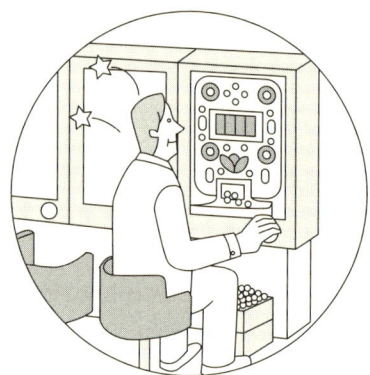

With shorter work hours and a 5-day work week, Japanese have more free time than ever before. Not surprisingly, the demand for leisure services is growing. For example, in 2000 the number of Japanese vacationing abroad reached an all-time high. New sales methods using the Internet are very important to the many changes we see in today's leisure industry.

The overseas travel boom

The number of Japanese traveling to overseas destinations reached 10 million in 1990. Afterwards the numbers grew slowly because of the recession. Soon after, however, appreciation of the yen stimulated more overseas travel, and travelers to overseas destinations reached 17 million in 2000. In a recent survey of what business persons consider to be their most important activities in life, 65% of respondents listed hobbies or non-work interests, — while 50% said work. Among non-work interests, travel ranked second in popularity. So there is still a tremendous, untapped potential demand for travel-related services.

On the other hand, travel within Japan has been affected by the recession-caused slump in disposable consumer income. In 1999 the number of Japanese who spent more than one night on domestic trips was 4.4% less than the previous year. Nevertheless, there is a continuing rush to open new hotels in spite of the recession. Older, well-known hotels are affected by this competition, of course, and many are finding themselves displaced.

IT causes big changes

While Japan's travel industry seems posed for continued growth, the Internet is having some interesting effects. As convenient 'Net sales' expand, consumers can buy plane tickets and make hotel reservations directly. Needless to say, the travel agencies are uneasy about decreased commissions, which have been the source of their livelihood. As a countermeasure, they are putting together innovative and specialized travel packages, rather than relying wholly on commissions.

The hotel industry, however, can cut costs on orders taken directly over the Internet, to the benefit of consumers. And this is giving rise to new price-cutting competition among hotels, even traditional Japanese inns. More and more hotels are making efforts to introduce new plans, such as day-use, barrier-free, and so on.

Amusement, from theme park to *pachinko* parlor

Older game arcades are going high-tech, and large amusement parks, which also tend to incorporate a lot of electronic gadgetry, are especially popular among the young video game generation.

On the other hand, with the exception of Tokyo Disneyland, changing times and consumer tastes are causing decreased attendance at theme parks, which required enormous investments and cost a great deal to maintain. Some say more than 70% of all theme parks are in financial difficulty.

Universal Studio Japan in Osaka, built in 2001, is expected to be an exception — another success of theme park in Japan besides Disneyland.

Other players in Japan's amusement industry that can't go unmentioned are *pachinko* and karaoke. Both are popular among young and old, but their markets have shrunk recently.

Pachinko, the popular pastime that originated with pinball machines from the United States, uses high-precision, computerized machines today. Although on the gray side of the law, prizes won from *pachinko* parlors can be exchanged for cash at special broker windows, one reason *pachinko* has grown into an enormous 20-trillion yen industry. Today *pachinko* parlors try to extend the market to the women and the elderly.

Good to know

Participation in leisurely activities

(Unit: thousand)　　　　(¥)

	Activity	No. of participants	Average one-time expenditure
1	Dinning out	71,300	3,870
2	Leisurely drive	60,400	2,100
3	Domestic travel	56,000	34,320
4	Karaoke	50,600	1,480
5	Watching videos (including rental)	49,400	460
6	Listening to music (CDs, records, etc.)	43,000	210
7	Gardening	40,500	490
8	Visiting zoos, botanical gardens, aquariums, museums	39,200	3,380
9	Bars and pubs	38,200	5,130
10	Lottery	36,300	3,640

Source: Leisure Development Center

APPENDIX 1

Major Company Directory by Industry ⒿJapanese information only

1. Software

● 任天堂　　　　　　　　　　Nintendo of America Inc.
　　　　　　　　http://www.nintendo.com/index.jsp

● セガ　　　　　　　　　　　SEGA Enterprises, Ltd.
　　　　　　　　http://www.sega.co.jp/home_e.html

● ソフトバンク　　　　　　　Softbank Corp.
　　　　　　　　http://www.softbank.co.jp/e_top

● 富士ソフトABC　　　　　　Fujisoft ABC Inc.
　　　　　　　　http://www.fsi.co.jp/company_e/index_sa1.html

● ソースネクスト　　　　　　Sourcenext Corp.
　　　　　　　　http://www.sourcenext.com/e/

● スクウェア　　　　　　　　Square Co., Ltd.
　　　　　　　　http://ir.square.co.jp/e/index.html

● ジャストシステム　　　　　Justsystem Corp.
　　　　　　　　http://www.justsystem.com/

● 住友金属システムソリューションズ　Sumitomo Metal System Solutions Co., Ltd.
　　　　　　　　http://www.smisol.co.jp/company/message_en.html

2. Household Appliance

● ソニー　　　　　　　　　　Sony Corp.
　　　　　　　　http://www.world.sony.com/

● 松下電器産業　　　　　　　Matsushita Electric Industrial Co., Ltd.
　　　　　　　　http://www.panasonic.co.jp/global/top.html

● NEC　　　　　　　　　　　NEC Corp.
　　　　　　　　http://www.nec.com/

● シャープ　　　　　　　　　Sharp Corp.
　　　　　　　　http://sharp-world.com/index.html

● キヤノン　　　　　　　　　Canon Inc.
　　　　　　　　http://www.canon.com/index.html

● 富士通　　　　　　　　　　Fujitsu Ltd.
　　　　　　　　http://www.fujitsu.com/

● 三洋電機　　　　　　　　　Sanyo Electric Co., Ltd.
　　　　　　　　http://www.sanyo.co.jp/koho/index_e.html

● 日立製作所　　　　　　　　Hitachi, Ltd.
　　　　　　　　http://global.hitachi.com/

● カシオ計算機　　　　　　　Casio Computer Co., Ltd.
　　　　　　　　http://world.casio.com/

● マブチモーター　　　　　　Mabuchi Motor Co., Ltd.
　　　　　　　　http://www.mabuchi-motor.co.jp/english/index.html

3. Automobiles and Motorcycles

● トヨタ自動車　　　　　　　Toyota Motor Corp.
　　　　　　　　http://www.global.toyota.com/

●本田技研工業   Honda Motor Co., Ltd.
                                      http://world.honda.com/
●日産自動車   Nissan Motor Co., Ltd.
                                      http://www.nissan-global.com/EN/HOME/index.html
●三菱自動車   Mitsubishi Motors Corp.
                                      http://www.mitsubishi-motors.co.jp/inter/entrance.html
●マツダ   Mazda Motor Corp.
                                      http://www.mazda.com/normal.html
●いすゞ自動車   Isuzu Motors Ltd.
                                      http://www.isuzu.co.jp/world/index.htm
●スズキ   Suzuki Motor Corp.
                                      http://www.suzuki.co.jp/cpd/koho_e/index.htm
●富士重工業   Fuji Heavy Industries Ltd.
                                      http://www.fhi.co.jp/english/index.htm
●日野自動車   Hino Motors, Ltd.
                                      http://www.hino.co.jp/index_e.html
●ダイハツ工業   Daihatsu Motor Co., Ltd.
                                        http://www.ingway.co.jp/~daihatsu/
●デンソー   Denso Corp.
                                      http://www.denso.co.jp/index-e.html

4. Petrochemical

●住友化学工業   Sumitomo Chemical Co., Ltd.
                                      http://www.sumitomo-chem.co.jp/menuE.html
●三菱化学   Mitsubishi Chemical Corp.
                                      http://www.m-kagaku.co.jp/index_en.htm
●積水化学工業   Sekisui Chemical Co., Ltd.
                                      http://www.sekisui.co.jp/general/english/index.html
●三井化学   Mitsui Chemicals, Inc.
                                      http://www.mitsui-chem.co.jp/english/index.htm
●信越化学工業   Shin-Etsu Chemical Co., Ltd.
                                      http://www.shinetsu.co.jp/english/index.html

5. Medical and Pharmaceutical

●武田薬品工業   Takeda Chemical Industries, Ltd.
                                      http://www.takeda.co.jp/index-e.html
●三共   Sankyo Co., Ltd.
                                      http://www.sankyo.co.jp/menu_e.html
●山之内製薬   Yamanouchi Pharmaceutical Co., Ltd.
                                      http://www.yamanouchi.com/eg/index.html
●大正製薬   Taisho Pharmaceutical Co., Ltd.
                                      http://www.taisho.co.jp/outline/index-e.htm
●第一製薬   Daiichi Pharmaceutical Co., Ltd.
                                      http://www.daiichipharm.co.jp/index-e.html
●小野薬品工業   Ono Pharmaceutical Co., Ltd.
                                      http://www.ono.co.jp/index.html
●エーザイ   Eisai Co., Ltd.
                                      http://www.eisai.co.jp/index-e.html

●中外製薬   Chugai Pharmaceutical Co., Ltd.
          http://www.chugai-pharm.co.jp/ceind02/index.htm

●ツムラ   Tsumura & Co.
          http://www.tsumura.co.jp/english/index.htm

●塩野義製薬   Shionogi & Co., Ltd.
          http://www.shionogi.co.jp/ — **ⓙ**

6. Textile

●日本ユニパックホールディング Nippon Unipac Holding
          http://www.nipponunipac.com/e/index.html

●王子製紙   Oji Paper Co., Ltd.
          http://www.ojipaper.co.jp/english/index.html

●大王製紙   Daio Paper Corp.
          http://www.daio-paper.co.jp/ — **ⓙ**

●レンゴー   Rengo Co., Ltd.
          http://www.rengo.co.jp/ — **ⓙ**

●東レ   Toray Industries, Inc.
          http://www.toray.co.jp/e/index.html

●帝人   Teijin Ltd.
          http://www.teijin.co.jp/english/flash.html

●カネボウ   Kanebo, Ltd.
          http://www.kanebo.co.jp/english/Index.htm

●東洋紡績   Toyobo Co., Ltd.
          http://www.toyobo.co.jp/e/index.htm

7. Steel and Nonferrous Metals

●新日本製鐵   Nippon Steel Corp.
          http://www.nsc.co.jp/english/index.html

●ＮＫＫ   NKK Corp.
          http://www.nkk.co.jp/en/index.html

●住友金属工業   Sumitomo Metal Industries, Ltd.
          http://www.sumikin.co.jp/e/index.html

●川崎製鉄   Kawasaki Steel Corp.
          http://www.kawasaki-steel.co.jp/index_e.html

●東洋製罐   Toyo Seikan Kaisha Ltd.

●トステム   Tostem Corp.
          http://www.tostem.co.jp/ — **ⓙ**

●住友電気工業   Sumitomo Electric Industries, Ltd.
          http://www.sei.co.jp/welcome_e.html

●古河電気工業   Furukawa Electric Co., Ltd.
          http://www.furukawa.co.jp/english/cover.htm

8. Machine

●三菱重工業   Mitsubishi Heavy Industries, Ltd.
          http://www.mhi.co.jp/Welcome.html

●リコー   Ricoh Co., Ltd.
          http://www.ricoh.com/

●コマツ	Komatsu Ltd.
	http://www.komatsu.com/
●クボタ	Kubota Corp.
	http://www.kubota.co.jp/english/index.html
●住友重機械工業	Sumitomo Heavy Industries, Ltd.
	http://www.shi.co.jp/english/index.html
●オリンパス光学工業	Olympus Optical Co., Ltd.
	http://www.olympus.co.jp/indexE.html
●ミノルタ	Minolta Co., Ltd.
	http://www.minolta.com/
●シチズン電子	Citizen Electronics Co., Ltd.
	http://www.c-e.co.jp/english/index.html
●セイコー	Seiko Corp.
	http://www.seiko-corp.co.jp/index_e.html

9. Food and Agricultural Products

●雪印乳業	Snow Brand Milk Products Co., Ltd.
	http://www.snowbrand.co.jp/index.htm
●キリンビール	Kirin Brewery Co., Ltd.
	http://www1.kirin.co.jp/english/
●アサヒビール	Asahi Breweries, Ltd.
	http://www.asahibeer.co.jp/english/index.htm
●味の素	Ajinomoto Co., Inc.
	http://www.ajinomoto.com/
●山崎製パン	Yamazaki Baking Co., Ltd.
	http://www.yamazakipan.co.jp/ — ❶
●日清食品	Nissin Food Products Co., Ltd.
	http://www.nissinfoods.co.jp/english/
●ニチレイ	Nichirei Corp.
	http://www.nichirei.co.jp/english/index.html
●キユーピー	Q.P. Corp.
	http://www.kewpie.co.jp/english/index.html
●JT	Japan Tobacco Inc.
	http://www.jtnet.ad.jp/WWW/JT/JTI_E/Welcome.html
●キッコーマン	Kikkoman Corp.
	http://www.kikkoman.com/
●日本水産	Nippon Suisan Kaisha, Ltd. (NISSUI)
	http://www.nissui.co.jp/top.html — ❶
●マルハ	Maruha Corp.
	http://www.maruha.co.jp/ — ❶

10. Banking & Securities

●三井住友銀行	Sumitomo Mitsui Banking Corp.
	http://www.smbc.co.jp/global/
●三菱東京フィナンシャル・グループ	Mitsubishi Tokyo Financial Group, Inc.
	http://www.mtfg.co.jp/english/index.html
●みずほフィナンシャルグループ	Mizuho Financial Group
	http://www.mizuho-fg.co.jp/eng/index.html

●UFJホールディングス　　　UFJ Holdings, Inc.
　　　　　　　　　　　　　　　http://www.ufj.co.jp/renew/english/index.html
●大和証券グループ本社　　　Daiwa Securities Group Inc.
　　　　　　　　　　　　　　　http://www.ir.daiwa.co.jp/default_english.asp
●日興證券　　　　　　　　　The Nikko Securities Co., Ltd.
　　　　　　　　　　　　　　　http://www.nikko.co.jp/SEC/e_home.html
●野村證券　　　　　　　　　The Nomura Securities Co., Ltd.
　　　　　　　　　　　　　　　http://www.nomura.co.jp/e/index.html

11. Wholesaling and Retailing

●セブン－イレブン・ジャパン　Seven-Eleven Japan Co., Ltd.
　　　　　　　　　　　　　　　http://sej.gsc.ne.jp/10/index.html
●ローソン　　　　　　　　　Lawson, Inc.
　　　　　　　　　　　　　　　http://www.lawson.co.jp/ — Ⓙ
●ファミリーマート　　　　　Family Mart Co., Ltd.
　　　　　　　　　　　　　　　http://www.family.co.jp/inf/gaiyo_e.html
●イトーヨーカ堂　　　　　　Ito-Yokado Co., Ltd.
　　　　　　　　　　　　　　　http://www.itoyokado.iyg.co.jp/iy/index1_e.htm
●ダイエー　　　　　　　　　The Daiei, Inc.
　　　　　　　　　　　　　　　http://www.daiei.co.jp/ — Ⓙ
●ジャスコ　　　　　　　　　Jusco Co., Ltd.
　　　　　　　　　　　　　　　http://www.jusco.co.jp/koho/index_e.html
●良品計画　　　　　　　　　Ryohin Keikaku Co., Ltd.
　　　　　　　　　　　　　　　http://www.muji.co.jp/en/index.html
●ファーストリテイリング　　Fast Retailing Co., Ltd.
　　　　　　　　　　　　　　　http://www.uniqlo.co.jp/index03.htm — Ⓙ
●すかいらーく　　　　　　　Skylark Co., Ltd.
　　　　　　　　　　　　　　　http://www.skylark.co.jp/
●吉野屋ディー・アンド・シー　Yoshinoya D&C Co., Ltd.
　　　　　　　　　　　　　　　http://www.yoshinoya-dc.com/eng/n_top.html
●マツモトキヨシ　　　　　　Matsumotokiyoshi Co., Ltd.
　　　　　　　　　　　　　　　http://www.matsukiyo.co.jp/noflash.html — Ⓙ

12. General Trading

●三菱商事　　　　　　　　　Mitsubishi Corp.
　　　　　　　　　　　　　　　http://www.mitsubishi.co.jp/En/index_top.html
●住友商事　　　　　　　　　Sumitomo Corp.
　　　　　　　　　　　　　　　http://www.sumitomocorp.co.jp/index-e.html
●三井物産　　　　　　　　　Mitsui & Co., Ltd.
　　　　　　　　　　　　　　　http://www.mitsui.co.jp/tkabz/english/index.htm
●日商岩井　　　　　　　　　Nissho Iwai Corp.
　　　　　　　　　　　　　　　http://www.nisshoiwai.co.jp/ni/e/index.html
●サンリオ　　　　　　　　　Sanrio Co., Ltd.
　　　　　　　　　　　　　　　http://www.sanrio.co.jp/english/welcome.html
●オートバックスセブン　　　Autobacs Seven Co., Ltd.
　　　　　　　　　　　　　　　http://www.autobacs-seven.com/visual_ver/en/index.html
●日本ユニシス　　　　　　　Nihon Unisys, Ltd.
　　　　　　　　　　　　　　　http://www.unisys.co.jp/welcome-e.html

●菱食　　　　　　　　　　　Ryoshoku Ltd.
　　　　　　　　　　　　　　http://www.ryoshoku.co.jp/atop.html — **J**

13. Construction and Housing

●鹿島建設　　　　　　　　Kajima Corp.
　　　　　　　　　　　　　　http://www.kajima.co.jp/welcome.html
●大成建設　　　　　　　　Taisei Corp.
　　　　　　　　　　　　　　http://www.taisei.co.jp/english/index.html
●清水建設　　　　　　　　Shimizu Corp.
　　　　　　　　　　　　　　http://www.shimz.co.jp/english/index.html
●住友林業　　　　　　　　Sumitomo Forestry Co., Ltd.
　　　　　　　　　　　　　　http://www.sfc.co.jp/esumi.htm
●大東建託　　　　　　　　Daito Trust Construction Co., Ltd.
　　　　　　　　　　　　　　http://www.kentaku.co.jp/English.html
●積水ハウス　　　　　　　Sekisui House, Ltd.
　　　　　　　　　　　　　　http://www.sekisuihouse.co.jp/english/index.html
●大和ハウス工業　　　　　Daiwa House Industry Co., Ltd.
　　　　　　　　　　　　　　http://www.daiwahouse.co.jp/welcome.html
●ミサワホーム　　　　　　Misawa Homes Co., Ltd.
　　　　　　　　　　　　　　http://www.misawa.co.jp/ — **J**
●大林組　　　　　　　　　Obayashi Corp.
　　　　　　　　　　　　　　http://www.obayashi.co.jp/english/index.html

14. Transportation

●東日本旅客鉄道　　　　　East Japan Railway Co.
　　　　　　　　　　　　　　http://www.jreast.co.jp/e/index.html
●東海旅客鉄道　　　　　　Central Japan Railway Co.
　　　　　　　　　　　　　　http://www.jr-central.co.jp/info_e.nsf/frame/corp-infomenu_e
●西日本旅客鉄道　　　　　West Japan Railway Co.
　　　　　　　　　　　　　　http://www.westjr.co.jp/kou/english/index_e.html
●日本通運　　　　　　　　Nippon Express Co., Ltd. (NITTSU)
　　　　　　　　　　　　　　http://www.nittsu.co.jp/english/e_index.htm
●ヤマト運輸　　　　　　　Yamato Transport Co., Ltd.
　　　　　　　　　　　　　　http://www.kuronekoyamato.co.jp/english/index.html
●日本郵船　　　　　　　　Nippon Yusen Kabushiki Kaisha (NYK Line)
　　　　　　　　　　　　　　http://www.nykline.co.jp/english/main.htm
●日本航空　　　　　　　　Japan Airlines Co., Ltd. (JAL)
　　　　　　　　　　　　　　http://www.jal.co.jp/e/index.html
●日本エアシステム　　　　Japan Air System Co., Ltd. (JAS)
　　　　　　　　　　　　　　http://www.jas.co.jp/E_JASHOM.htm
●全日本空輸　　　　　　　All Nippon Airways Co., Ltd. (ANA)
　　　　　　　　　　　　　　http://www.ana.co.jp/eng/index.html

15. Communications

●ＮＴＴ　　　　　　　　　Nippon Telegraph and Telephone Corp.
　　　　　　　　　　　　　　http://www.ntt.co.jp/index_e.html
●ＮＴＴコミュニケーションズ　NTT Communications Corp.
　　　　　　　　　　　　　　http://www.ntt.com/index-e.html

●ＮＴＴドコモ　　　　　　　NTT DoCoMo, Inc.
　　　　　　　　　　　　　　http://www.nttdocomo.com/top.shtml
●ＫＤＤＩ　　　　　　　　　KDDI Corp.
　　　　　　　　　　　　　　http://www.kddi.com/english/index.html
●日本テレコム　　　　　　　Japan Telecom Co., Ltd.
　　　　　　　　　　　　　　http://www.japan-telecom.co.jp/index_e.html
●東京通信ネットワーク　　　Tokyo Telecomunication Network Co., Inc. (TTNet)
　　　　　　　　　　　　　　http://www.ttnet.co.jp/english/default.htm

16. Mass Communications

●日本テレビ放送網　　　　　Nippon Television Network Corp.
　　　　　　　　　　　　　　http://www.ntv.co.jp/english/
●フジテレビジョン　　　　　Fuji Television Network, Inc.
　　　　　　　　　　　　　　http://www.fujitv.co.jp/en/index.html
●東京放送　　　　　　　　　Tokyo Broadcasting System, Inc. (TBS)
　　　　　　　　　　　　　　http://www.tbs.co.jp/index.html
●日本放送協会　　　　　　　Japan Broadcasting Corp. (NHK)
　　　　　　　　　　　　　　http://www.nhk.or.jp/index-e.html
●朝日放送　　　　　　　　　Asahi Broadcasting Corp. (ABC)
　　　　　　　　　　　　　　http://www.asahi.co.jp/abcHomeE.html
●講談社　　　　　　　　　　Kodansha, Ltd.
　　　　　　　　　　　　　　http://www.kodansha.co.jp/English/
●小学館　　　　　　　　　　Shogakukan, Inc.
　　　　　　　　　　　　　　http://skygarden.shogakukan.co.jp/sol/ENGLISH/index.html
●朝日新聞社　　　　　　　　Asahi Shimbun Publishing Co.
　　　　　　　　　　　　　　http://www.asahi.com/english/english.html
●読売新聞社　　　　　　　　The Yomiuri Shimbun
　　　　　　　　　　　　　　http://www.yomiuri.co.jp/index-e.htm
●日本経済新聞社　　　　　　Nihon Keizai Shimbun, Inc.
　　　　　　　　　　　　　　http://www.nni.nikkei.co.jp/

17. Leisure

●東京ディズニーランド　　　Tokyo Disneyland
　　　　　　　　　　　　　　http://www.tokyodisneyland.co.jp/index_e.html
●ユニバーサル・スタジオ・ジャパン　Universal Studios Japan
　　　　　　　　　　　　　　http://www.usj.co.jp/en/index1.html
●ＪＴＢ　　　　　　　　　　JTB Corp.
　　　　　　　　　　　　　　http://www.jtb.co.jp/eng/index.html
●エイチ・アイ・エス　　　　H.I.S. Co., Ltd.
　　　　　　　　　　　　　　http://www.his-j.com/tyo/air_eng/index_e.htm
●近畿日本ツーリスト　　　　Kinki Nippon Tourist Co., Ltd
　　　　　　　　　　　　　　http://www.knt.co.jp/kokusai/top.htm
●帝国ホテル　　　　　　　　Imperial Hotel, Ltd.
　　　　　　　　　　　　　　http://www.imperialhotel.co.jp/english/menu.html
●ホテルオークラ　　　　　　Hotel Okura Co., Ltd
　　　　　　　　　　　　　　http://www.okura.com/

APPENDIX 2

Business Information Sources

Business Information

Private Think Tanks
- ●Dentsu Institute for Human Studies （電通総研）
  http://www.dihs.dentsu.co.jp/english/index.html
- ●Hakuhodo Institute of Life and Living （博報堂生活総研）
  http://www.athill.com/english/e_menu.html
- ●Nomura Research Institute （野村総合研究所）
  http://www.nri.co.jp/english/index.html
- ●Daiwa Institute of Research （大和総研）
  http://www.dir.co.jp/Reception/welcome.html
- ●FUJI Research Institute （富士総合研究所）
  http://www.fuji-ric.co.jp/e_index.html
- ●Mitsubishi Research Institute （三菱総合研究所）
  http://www.mri.co.jp/E/index.html
- ●Sanwa Research Institute and Consulting （三和総合研究所　SRIC）
  http://www.sric.co.jp/eng/
- ●NLI Research Institute （ニッセイ基礎研究所）
  http://www.nli-research.co.jp/eng/index-e.html
- ●JMR Lifestyle Research Institute （JMR生活総合研究所）
  http://www.jmrlsi.co.jp/english/index.html
- ●The Japan Research Institute （日本総研）
  http://www.jri.co.jp/english/index.html

News
- ●NIKKEI NET Interactive - Business News （日本経済新聞社　NIKKEI NET）
  http://www.nni.nikkei.co.jp/
- ●Nikkei BP AsiaBizTech （日経BP社）
  http://www.asiabiztech.com/
- ●Toyo Keizai Web （東洋経済新報社）
  http://www.toyokeizai.co.jp/english/index.html
- ●PRESIDENT ONLINE （プレジデント社）
  http://www.president.co.jp/pre/english.html

Others
- ●Japan Credit Rating Agency （日本格付研究所）
  http://www.jcr.co.jp/homepagee.htm
- ●The Bank of Japan （日本銀行）
  http://www.boj.or.jp/en/index.htm
- ●Small and Medium Enterprise Information of Japan （日本の中小企業情報）
  http://www.sme.ne.jp/japane.html
- ●Japan Motor Industrial Federation （自動車工業振興会）
  http://www.motorshow.or.jp/eng/index.html

●US-Japan Technology Management Center （日米技術経営研究）
   http://fuji.stanford.edu/
●Electronic Commerce Promotion Council of Japan （電子商取引推進協議会　ECOM）
   http://www.ecom.or.jp/ecom_e/index.html
●Electronic Commerce Research Project （電子商取引研究プロジェクト　ECRP）
   http://www.ecrp.org/english/ecrp_e.html
●Global Information （グローバルインフォメーション）
   http://www.gii.co.jp/index_en.shtml

Government Ministries and Agencies

●Cabinet Office （内閣府）
   http://www.cao.go.jp/index-e.html
●The Kantei (Official Residence) of the Prime Minister of Japan （首相官邸）
   http://www.kantei.go.jp/foreign/index-e.html
●Financial Services Agency （金融庁）
   http://www.fsa.go.jp/indexe.html
●Ministry of Agriculture, Forestry and Fisheries of Japan （農林水産省）
   http://www.maff.go.jp/eindex.html
●Ministry of Economy, Trade and Industry （経済産業省）
   http://www.meti.go.jp/english/index.html
●Ministry of Education, Culture, Sports, Science and Technology （文部科学省）
   http://www.sta.go.jp/english/index.htm
●Ministry of Finance （財務省）
   http://www.mof.go.jp/english/index.htm
●Ministry of Health, Labor and Welfare （厚生労働省）
   http://www.mhlw.go.jp/english/index.html
●Ministry of Land, Infrastructure and Transport （国土交通省）
   http://www.mlit.go.jp/english/index.html
●Ministry of Public Management, Home Affairs, Posts and Telecommunications （総務省）
   http://www.soumu.go.jp/english/index.htm
●Ministry of the Environment （環境省）
   http://www.env.go.jp/en/index.html

Public Agencies

●Economic and Social Research Institute （経済社会総合研究所）
   http://www.esri.cao.go.jp/index-e.html
●Research Institute of Economy, Trade and Industry （経済産業研究所）
   http://www.rieti.go.jp/
●National Institute of Advanced Industrial Science and Technology （産業技術総合研究所）
   http://www.aist.go.jp/index.html
●National Space Development Agency of Japan （宇宙開発事業団　NASDA）
   http://www.nasda.go.jp/index_e.html

- ●National Aerospace Laboratory （航空宇宙技術研究所）
  http://www.nal.go.jp/Welcome-e.html
- ●Japan Science and Technology （科学技術振興事業団）
  http://www.jst.go.jp/EN/
- ●Communications Research Laboratory （通信総合研究所）
  http://www.crl.go.jp/overview/index.html
- ●Information-technology Promotion Agency, Japan （情報処理振興事業協会）
  http://www.ipa.go.jp/index_e.html
- ●Japan Marine Science and Technology Center （海洋科学技術センター）
  http://www.jamstec.go.jp/jamstec-e/index-e.html
- ●National Institute for Environmental Studies （国立環境研究所）
  http://www.nies.go.jp/index.html
- ●Japan Atomic Energy Research Institute （日本原子力研究所）
  http://www.jaeri.go.jp/english/index.cgi
- ●Agriculture, Forestry and Fisheries Research Council Secretariat （農林水産技術会議事務局）
  http://www.affrc.go.jp/index.html
- ●Japan External Trade Organization （日本貿易振興会　JETRO）
  http://www.jetro.go.jp/top/index.html
- ●Institute of Developing Economies （日本貿易振興会　アジア経済研究所　IDE-JETRO）
  http://www.ide.go.jp/English/index4.html
- ●Statistics Bureau & Statistics Center （総務省統計局・統計センター）
  http://www.stat.go.jp/english/1.htm

Economic Organizations / Chamber of Commerce

- ●Keidanren （経団連）
  http://www.keidanren.or.jp/index.html
- ●Japan Association of Corporate Executives （経済同友会）
  http://www.doyukai.or.jp/E_index.htm
- ●Japan Chamber of Commerce & Industry （日本商工会議所　JCCI）
  http://www.jcci.or.jp/home-e.html
- ●Nikkeiren （日経連）
  http://www.nikkeiren.or.jp

Hiragana/Katakana/Rōmaji

あ	い	う	え	お
ア	イ	ウ	エ	オ
a	i	u	e	o
か	き	く	け	こ
カ	キ	ク	ケ	コ
ka	ki	ku	ke	ko
さ	し	す	せ	そ
サ	シ	ス	セ	ソ
sa	shi	su	se	so
た	ち	つ	て	と
タ	チ	ツ	テ	ト
ta	chi	tsu	te	to
な	に	ぬ	ね	の
ナ	ニ	ヌ	ネ	ノ
na	ni	nu	ne	no
は	ひ	ふ	へ	ほ
ハ	ヒ	フ	ヘ	ホ
ha	hi	fu	he	ho
ま	み	む	め	も
マ	ミ	ム	メ	モ
ma	mi	mu	me	mo
や	(い)	ゆ	(え)	よ
ヤ	(イ)	ユ	(エ)	ヨ
ya	(i)	yu	(e)	yo
ら	り	る	れ	ろ
ラ	リ	ル	レ	ロ
ra	ri	ru	re	ro
わ	(い)	(う)	(え)	を
ワ	(イ)	(ウ)	(エ)	ヲ
wa	(i)	(u)	(e)	o
ん				
ン				
n				

が	ぎ	ぐ	げ	ご
ガ	ギ	グ	ゲ	ゴ
ga	gi	gu	ge	go
ざ	じ	ず	ぜ	ぞ
ザ	ジ	ズ	ゼ	ゾ
za	ji	zu	ze	zo
だ	ぢ	づ	で	ど
ダ	ヂ	ヅ	デ	ド
da	ji	zu	de	do
ば	び	ぶ	べ	ぼ
バ	ビ	ブ	ベ	ボ
ba	bi	bu	be	bo
ぱ	ぴ	ぷ	ぺ	ぽ
パ	ピ	プ	ペ	ポ
pa	pi	pu	pe	po

きゃ	きゅ	きょ	りゃ	りゅ	りょ
キャ	キュ	キョ	リャ	リュ	リョ
kya	kyu	kyo	rya	ryu	ryo
しゃ	しゅ	しょ	ぎゃ	ぎゅ	ぎょ
シャ	シュ	ショ	ギャ	ギュ	ギョ
sha	shu	sho	gya	gyu	gyo
ちゃ	ちゅ	ちょ	じゃ	じゅ	じょ
チャ	チュ	チョ	ジャ	ジュ	ジョ
cha	chu	cho	ja	ju	jo
にゃ	にゅ	にょ	びゃ	びゅ	びょ
ニャ	ニュ	ニョ	ビャ	ビュ	ビョ
nya	nyu	nyo	bya	byu	byo
ひゃ	ひゅ	ひょ	ぴゃ	ぴゅ	ぴょ
ヒャ	ヒュ	ヒョ	ピャ	ピュ	ピョ
hya	hyu	hyo	pya	pyu	pyo
みゃ	みゅ	みょ			
ミャ	ミュ	ミョ			
mya	myu	myo			

William(Bill) Carter is a historian, writer and translator. He has lived in Japan for many years and is a fluent speaker of Japanese. He has studied at Massachusetts Institute of Technology, Harvard University, and the University of Tokyo. His interests include intercultural communications, anthropology, politics and peace research. He is a member of the International Peace Research Association (IPRA). His translation work includes Postwar Politician: The Life of Former Prime Minister Masayoshi Ohira, Japan's Contribution to the World (Kodansha International) and Guide to the Aska Historical Museum.